Farewell Love!

A N

Matilde Serao

Alpha Editions

This edition published in 2021

ISBN : 9789355754769

Design and Setting By
Alpha Editions
www.alphaedis.com
Email - info@alphaedis.com

INTRODUCTION

The most prominent imaginative writer of the latest generation in Italy is a woman. What little is known of the private life of Matilde Serao (Mme. Scarfoglio) adds, as forcibly as what may be divined from the tenour and material of her books, to the impression that every student of literary history must have formed of the difficulties which hem in the intellectual development of an ambitious girl. Without unusual neglect, unusual misfortune, it seems impossible for a woman to arrive at that experience which is essential to the production of work which shall be able to compete with the work of the best men. It is known that the elements of hardship and enforced adventure have not been absent from the career of the distinguished Italian novelist. Madame Serao has learned in the fierce school of privation what she teaches to us with so much beauty and passion in her stories.

Matilde Serao was born on the 17th of March 1856, in the little town of Patras, on the western coast of Greece. Her father, Francisco Serao, was a Neapolitan political exile, her mother a Greek princess, the last survivor of an ancient noble family. I know not under what circumstances she came to the Italian home of her father, but it was probably in 1861 or soon afterwards that the unification of Italy permitted his return. At an early age, however, she seems to have been left without resources. She received a rough education at the Scuola Normale in Naples, and she obtained a small clerkship in the telegraph office at Rome.

Literature, however, was the profession she designed to excel in, and she showed herself a realist at once. Her earliest story, if I do not mistake, was that minute picture of the vicissitudes of a post-office which is named *Telegraphi dello Stato* ("State Telegraphs"). She worked with extreme energy, she taught herself shorthand, and in 1878 she quitted the post-office to become a reporter and a journalist. To give herself full scope in this new employment, she, as I have been assured, cut short her curly crop of hair, and adopted on occasion male costume. She soon gained a great proficiency in reporting, and advanced to the writing of short sketches and stories for the newspapers. The power and originality of these attempts were acknowledged, and the name of Matilde Serao gradually became one of those which irresistibly attracted public attention. The writer of these lines may be permitted to record the impression which more than ten years ago was made upon him by reading a Neapolitan sketch, signed by that then wholly obscure name, in a chance number of the Roman *Fanfulla*.

The short stories were first collected in a little volume in 1879. In 1880 Matilde Serao became suddenly famous by the publication of the charming story *Fantasia* ("Fantasy"), which has already been presented to an English public in the present series of translations. It was followed by a much weaker study of Neapolitan life, *Cuore Infermo* ("A Heart Diseased"). In 1881 she published "The Life and Adventures of Riccardo Joanna," to which she added a continuation in 1885. It is not possible to enumerate all Madame Serao's successive publications, but the powerful romance, *La Conquista di Roma* ("The Conquest of Rome"), 1882, must not be omitted. This is a very careful and highly finished study of bureaucratic ambition, admirably characterised. Since then she has written in rapid succession several volumes of collected short stories, dealing with the oddities of Neapolitan life, and a curious novel, "The Virtue of Cecchina," 1884. Her latest romances, most of them short, have been *Terno Secco* ("A Dry Third"), a very charming episode of Italian life, illustrating the frenzied interest taken in the public lotteries, 1887; *Addio Amore* ("Farewell Love!"), 1887, which is here, for the first time, published in English; *La Granda Fiamma*, 1889; and *Sogno di una notte d'estate* ("A Summer Night's Dream"), 1890.

The method of Matilde Serao's work, its qualities and its defects, can only be comprehended by those who realise that she came to literature through journalism. When she began life, in 1878, it was as a reporter, a paragraph-writer, a woman of all work on any Roman or Neapolitan newspaper which would give her employment. Later on, she founded and carried on a newspaper of her own, the *Corriere di Roma*. After publishing this lively sheet for a few years, she passed to Naples, and became the editor of *Le Corriere di Napoli*, the paper which enjoys the largest circulation of any journal in the south of Italy. She has married a journalist, Eduardo Scarfoglio, and all her life has been spent in ministering to the appetites of the vast, rough crowd that buys cheap Italian newspapers. Her novels have been the employment of her rare and broken leisure; they bear the stamp of the more constant business of her life.

The naturalism of Matilde Serao deserves to be distinguished from that of the French contemporaries with whom she is commonly classed. She has a fiercer passion, more of the true ardour of the South, than Zola or Maupassant, but her temperament is distinctly related to that of Daudet. She is an idealist working in the school of realism; she climbs, on scaffolding of minute prosaic observation, to heights which' are emotional and often lyrical. But her most obvious merit is the acuteness with which she has learned to collect and arrange in artistic form the elements of the town life of Southern Italy. She still retains in her nature something of the newspaper reporter's quicksilver, but it is sublimated by the genius of a poet.

EDMUND GOSSE.

PART I

I.

Motionless under the white coverlet of her bed, Anna appeared to have been sleeping soundly for the past two hours.

Her sister Laura, who occupied a little cot at the other end of the big room, had that evening much prolonged her customary reading, which followed the last gossip of the day between the girls. But no sooner had she put out her candle than Anna opened her eyes and fixed them upon Laura's bed, which glimmered vaguely white in the distance.

Anna was wide awake.

She dared not move, she dared not even sigh; and all her life was in her gaze, trying to penetrate the secret of the dusk—trying to see whether really her sister was asleep. It was a winter's night, and as the hour advanced the room became colder and colder; but Anna did not feel it.

The moment the light had been extinguished a flame had leapt from her heart to her brain, diffusing itself through all her members, scalding her veins, scorching her flesh, quickening the beating of her pulses. As in the height of fever, she felt herself burning up; her tongue was dry, her head was hot; and the icy air that entered her lungs could not quench the fire in her, could not subdue the tumultuous irruption of her young blood.

Often, to relieve herself, she had longed to cry out, to moan; but the fear of waking Laura held her silent. It was not, however, so much from the great heat throbbing at her temples that she suffered, as from her inability to know for certain whether her sister was asleep.

Sometimes she thought of moving noisily, so that her bed should creak; then if Laura was awake, she would move in hers, and thus Anna could make sure. But the fear of thereby still further lengthening this time of waiting, kept her from letting the thought become an action. She lay as motionless as if her limbs were bound down by a thousand chains.

She had lost all track of time, too; she had forgotten to count the last strokes of the clock—the clock that could be heard from the sitting-room adjoining. It seemed to her that she had been lying like this for years, that she had been waiting for years, burning with this maddening fire for years, that she had spent years trying to pierce the darkness with her eyes.

And then the horrible thought crossed her mind—What if the hour had passed? Perhaps it had passed without her noticing it; she who had waited for it so impatiently had let it escape.

But no. Presently, deadened by the distance and the doors closed between, she heard the clock ring out.

The hour had come.

Thereupon, with an infinite caution, born of infinite fear, slowly, trembling, holding her breath at every sound, pausing, starting back, going on, she sat up in bed, and at last slipped out of it.

That vague spot of whiteness in the distance, where her sister lay, still fascinated her; she kept her head turned in its direction, while with her hands she felt for her shoes and stockings and clothes. They were all there, placed conveniently near; but every little difficulty she had to overcome in dressing, so as not to make the slightest noise, represented a world of precautions, of pauses, and of paralysing fears.

When at last she had got on her frock of white serge, which shone out in the darkness, "Perhaps Laura sees me," she thought.

But she had made ready a big heavy black shawl, and in this she now wrapped herself from head to foot, and the whiteness of her frock was hidden.

Then, having accomplished the miracle of dressing herself, she stood still at her bedside; she had not dared to take a step as yet, sure that by doing so she would wake Laura.

"A little strength—Heaven send me a little strength," she prayed inwardly.

Then she set forth stealthily across the room. In the middle of it, seized by a sudden audacious impulse, she called her sister's name, in a whisper, "Laura, Laura," listening intensely.

No answer. She went on, past the door, through the sitting-room, the drawing-room, feeling her way amidst the chairs and tables. She struck her shoulder against the frame of the door between the sitting-room and the drawing-room, and halted for a moment, with a beating heart.

"*Madonna mia! Madonna mia!*" she murmured in an agony of terror.

Then she had to pass before the room of her governess, Stella Martini; but the poor, good lady was a sound sleeper, and Anna knew it.

When she reached the dining-room, it seemed to her that she must have traversed a hundred separate chambers, a hundred entire apartments, an endless chain of chambers and apartments.

At last she opened the door that gave upon the terrace, and ran out into the night, the cold, the blackness. She crossed the terrace to the low dividing-wall between it and the next.

"Giustino—Giustino," she called.

Suddenly the shadow of a man appeared on the other terrace, very near, very close to the wall of division.

A voice answered: "Here I am, Anna."

But she, taking his hand, drew him towards her, saying: "Come, come."

He leapt over the little wall.

Covered by her black mantle, without speaking, Anna bent her head and broke into sobs.

"What is it? What is wrong?" he asked, trying to see her face.

Anna wept without answering.

"Don't cry, don't cry. Tell me what's troubling you," he murmured earnestly, with a caress in his words and in his voice.

"Nothing, nothing. I was so frightened," she stammered.

"Dearest, dearest, dearest!" he whispered.

"Oh, I'm a poor creature—a poor thing," said she, with a desolate gesture.

"I love you so," said Giustino, simply, in a low voice.

"Oh, say that again," she begged, ceasing to weep.

"I love you so, Anna."

"I adore you—my soul, my darling."

"If you love me, you must be calm."

"I adore you, my dearest one."

"Promise me that you won't cry any more, then."

"I adore you, I adore you, I adore you!" she repeated, her voice heavy with emotion.

He did not speak. It seemed as if he could find no words fit for responding to such a passion. A cold gust of wind swept over them.

"Are you cold?" he asked.

"No: feel." And she gave him her hand.

Her little hand, between those of Giustino, was indeed not cold; it was burning.

"That is love," said she.

He lifted the hand gently to his lips, and kissed it lightly. And thereupon, her eyes glowed in the darkness, like human stars of passion.

"My love is consuming me," she went on, as if speaking to herself. "I can feel nothing else; neither cold, nor night, nor danger—nothing. I can only feel *you*. I want nothing but your love. I only want to live near you always—till death, and after death—always with you—always, always."

"Ah me!" sighed he, under his breath.

"What did you say?" she cried, eagerly.

"It was a sigh, dear one; a sigh over our dream."

"Don't talk like that; don't say that," she exclaimed.

"Why shouldn't I say it, Anna? The sweet dream that we have been dreaming together—any day we may have to wake from it. They aren't willing that we should live together."

"Who—they?"

"He who can dispose of you as he wishes, Cesare Dias."

"Have you seen him?"

"Yes; to-day."

"And he won't consent?"

"He won't consent."

"Why not?"

"Because you have money, and I have none. Because you are noble, and I'm not."

"But I adore you, Giustino."

"That matters little to your guardian."

"He's a bad man."

"He's a man," said Giustino, shortly.

"But it's an act of cruelty that he's committing," she cried, lifting her hands towards heaven.

Giustino did not speak.

"What did you answer? What did you plead? Didn't you tell him again that you love me, that I adore you, that I shall die if we are separated? Didn't you describe our despair to him?"

"It was useless," replied Giustino, sadly.

"Oh, dear! Oh, dear! You didn't tell him of our love, of our happiness? You didn't implore him, weeping? You didn't try to move his hard old heart? But what sort of man are you; what sort of soul have you, that you let them sentence us to death like this? O Lord! O Lord!—what man have I been loving?"

"Anna, Anna!" he said, softly.

"Why didn't you defy him? Why didn't you rebel? You're young; you're brave. How could Cesare Dias, almost an old man, with ice in his veins, how could he frighten you?"

"Because Cesare Dias was right, Anna," he answered quietly.

"Oh, horror! Horrible sacrilege of love!" cried Anna, starting back.

In her despair she had unconsciously allowed her shawl to drop from her shoulders; it had fallen to the ground, at her feet. And now she stood up before him like a white, desolate phantom, impelled by sorrow to wander the earth on a quest that can never have an end.

But he had a desperate courage, though it forced him to break with the only woman he had ever loved.

"Cesare Dias was right, my dearest Anna. I couldn't answer him. I'm a poor young fellow, without a farthing."

"Love is stronger than money."

"I am a commoner, I have no title to give you."

"Love is stronger than a title."

"Everything is against our union, Anna."

"Love is stronger than everything; stronger even than death."

After this there befell a silence. But he felt that he must go to the bottom of the subject. He saw his duty, and overcame his pain.

"Think a little, Anna. Our souls were made for each other; but our persons are placed in such different circumstances, separated by so many things, such great distances, that not even a miracle could unite them. You accuse me of being a traitor to our love, which is our strength; but is it unworthy of us to conquer ourselves in such a pass? Anna, Anna, it is I who lose everything; and yet I advise you to forget this youthful fancy. You are young; you are beautiful; you are rich; you are noble, and you love me; yet it is my duty to say to you, forget me—forget me. Consider how great the sacrifice is, and see if it is not our duty, as two good people, to make it courageously. Anna, you will be loved again, better still, by a better man. You deserve the purest and the noblest love. You won't be unhappy long. Life is still sweet for you. You weep, yes; you suffer; because you love me, because you are a dear, loving woman. But afterwards, afterwards you will find your path broad and flowery. It is I who will have nothing left; the light of my life will go out, the fire in my heart. But what does it matter? You will forget me, Anna."

Anna, motionless, listened to him, uttering no word.

"Speak," he said, anxiously.

"I can't forget you," she answered.

"Try—make the effort. Let us try not to see each other."

"No, no; it's useless," she said, her voice dying on her lips.

"What do you wish us to do?"

"I don't know. I don't know."

A great impulse of pity, greater than his own sorrow, assailed him. He took her hands; they were cold now.

"What is the matter with you? Are you ill?"

She did not answer. She leant her head on his shoulder, and he caressed her rich, brown hair.

"Anna, what is it?" he whispered, thrilled by a wild emotion.

"You don't love me."

"How can you doubt it?"

"If you loved me," she began, sobbing, "you would not propose our separation. If you loved me you would not think such a separation possible. If you loved me it would be like death to you to forget and be forgotten. Giustino, you don't love me."

"Anna, Anna!"

"Judge by me," she went on, softly. "I'm a poor, weak woman; yet I resist, I struggle. And we would conquer, we would conquer, if you loved me."

"Anna!"

"Ah, don't call my name; don't speak my name. All this tenderness—what's the use of it? It is good; it is wise; it is comforting. But it is only tenderness; it isn't love. You can think, reflect, determine. That isn't love. You speak of duty, of being worthy—worthy of her who adores you, who sees nothing but you in the whole wide world. I know nothing of all that. I love you. I know nothing. And only now I realise that your love isn't love. You are silent. I don't understand you. You can't understand me. Good-bye, love!"

She turned away from him, to move off. But he detained her.

"What do you want to do?" he whispered.

"If I can't live with you, I must die," she said, quietly, with her eyes closed, as if she were thus awaiting death.

"Don't speak of dying, Anna. Don't make my regret worse than it is. It's I who have spoiled your life."

"It doesn't matter."

"It's I who have put bitterness into your sweet youth."

"It doesn't matter."

"It's I who have stirred you up to rebel against Cesare Dias, against your sister Laura, against the wish of your parents and all your friends."

"It doesn't matter."

"It is I who have called you from your sleep, who have exposed you to a thousand dangers. Think, if you were discovered here you would be lost."

"It doesn't matter. Take me away."

And Giustino, in spite of the darkness, could see her fond eyes glowing.

"If you would only take me away," she sighed.

"But where?"

"Anywhere—to any country. You will be my country."

"Elope? A noble young girl—elope like an adventuress?"

"Love will secure my pardon."

"I will pardon you; no others will."

"You will be my family, my all. Take me away."

"Anna, Anna, where should we find refuge? Without means, without friends, having committed a great fault, our life would be most unhappy."

"No, no, no! Take me away. We'll have a little time of poverty, after which I shall get possession of my fortune. Take me away."

"And I shall be accused of having made a good speculation. No, no, Anna, it's impossible. I couldn't bear such a shame."

She started away from him, pushing him back with a movement of horror.

"What?" she cried. "What? You would be ashamed? It's your shame that preoccupies you? And mine? Honoured, esteemed, loved, I care nothing for this honour, this love, and am willing to lose all, the respect of people, the affection of my relations—and you think of yourself! I could have chosen any one of a multitude of young men of my own rank, my own set, and I have chosen you because you were good and honest and clever. And you are ashamed of what bad people and stupid people may say of you! I—I brave everything. I lie, I deceive. I leave my bed at the dead of night, steal out during my sister's sleep—out of my room, out of my house, like a guilty servant, so that they might call me the lowest of the low. I do all this to come to you; and you are thinking of speculations, of what the world will say about you. Oh, how strong you are, you men! How well you know your way; how straight you march, never listening to the voices that call to you, never feeling the hands that try to stop you—nothing, nothing, nothing! You are men, and have your honour to look after, your dignity to preserve, your delicate reputation to safeguard. You are right, you are reasonable. And so we are fools; we are mad, who step out of the path of honour and dignity for the love of you—we poor silly creatures of our hearts!"

Giustino had not attempted to protest against this outburst of violent language; but every word of it, hot with wrath, vibrant with sorrowful anger, stirred him to the quick, held him silenced, frightened, shaken by her voice, by the tumult of her passion. Now the fire which he had rashly kindled burnt up the whole beautiful, simple, stable edifice of his planning, and all he could see left of it was a smoking ruin. He loved her—she loved him; and though he knew it was wild and unreasonable. "Forgive me," he said; "let us go away."

She put her hand upon his head, and he heard her murmur, under her voice, "O God!"

They both felt that their life was decided, that they had played the grand stake of their existence.

There was a long pause; she was the first to break it.

"Listen, Giustino. Before we fly let me make one last attempt. You have spoken to Cesare Dias; you have told him that you love me, that I adore you; but he didn't believe you——"

"It is true. He smiled incredulously."

"He is a man who has seen a great deal of the world, who has been loved, who has loved; but of all that nothing is left to him. He is cold and solitary. He never speaks of his scepticism, but he believes in nothing. He's a miserable, arid creature. I know that he despises me, thinking me silly and enthusiastic. I pity him as I pity every one who has no love in his heart. And yet—I will speak to Cesare Dias. The truth will well up from me with such impetus that he cannot refuse to believe me. I'll tell him everything. In spite of his forty years, in spite of the corruption of his mind, in spite of all his scorn, all his irony, true love will find convincing words. He'll give his consent."

"Can't you first persuade your sister? There we'd have an affectionate ally," said Giustino, tentatively.

"My sister is worse than Cesare Dias," she answered, with a slight tremor of the voice; "I should never dare to depend on her."

"You are afraid of her?"

"Pray don't speak of her, don't speak of her. It's a subject which pains me."

"And yet——"

"No, no. Laura knows nothing; she must know nothing; it would be dreadful if she knew. I'd a thousand times rather speak to him. He will remember his past; Laura has no past—she has nothing—she's a dead soul. I will speak with him; he will believe me."

"And if he shouldn't believe you?"

"He *will* believe me."

"But, Anna, Anna, if he shouldn't?"

"Then—we will elope. But I ought to make this last attempt. Heaven will give me strength. Afterwards—I will write to you, I will tell you everything. I daren't come here any more. It's too dangerous. If any one should see me it would be the ruin of all our hopes. I'll write to you. You'll arrange your own affairs in the meantime—as if you were at the point of death, as if you were going to leave this country never to return. You must be ready at any instant."

"I'll be ready."

"Surely?"

"Surely."

"Without a regret?"

"Without a regret." But his voice died on his lips.

"Thank you; you love me. We shall be so happy! You will see. Happier than any one in the world!"

"So happy!" murmured Giustino, faithful but sad.

"And may Heaven help us," she concluded, fervently, putting out her hand to leave him.

He took her hand, and his pressure of it was a silent vow; but it was the vow of a friend, of a brother, simple and austere.

She moved slowly away, as if tired. He remained where he was, waiting a little before returning to his own terrace. Not until some ten minutes had passed, during which he heard no sound, no movement, could he feel satisfied that Anna had safely reached her room.

Once at home, he found himself used up, exhausted, without ideas, without emotions. And speedily he fell asleep.

She also was exhausted by the great moral crisis through which she had passed. An immense burden seemed to bow her down, to make heavy her footsteps, as she groped her way through the silent house.

When she reached the sitting-room she stopped with sudden terror. A light was burning in the bedroom. Laura would be awake, would have remarked her absence, would be waiting for her.

She stood still a long while. She could hear a sound as of the pages of a book being turned. Laura was reading.

At last she pushed open the door, and crossed the threshold.

Laura looked at her, smiled haughtily, and did not speak.

Anna fell on her knees before her, crying, "Forgive me. For pity's sake, Laura, forgive me. Laura, Laura, Laura!"

But the child remained silent, white and cold and virginal, never ceasing to smile scornfully.

Anna lay on the floor, weeping. And the winter dawn found her there, weeping, weeping; while her sister slept peacefully.

II.

The letter ran thus:

"DEAREST LOVE,—I have had my interview with Cesare Dias. What a man! His mere presence seemed to freeze me; it was enough if he looked at me, with his big clear blue eyes, for speech to fail me. There is something in his silence which frightens me; and when he speaks, his sharp voice quells me by its tone as well as by the hard things he says.

"And yet this morning when he came for his usual visit, I was bold enough to speak to him of my marriage. I spoke simply, briefly, without trembling, though I could see that the courtesy with which he listened was ironical. Laura was present, taciturn and absent-minded as usual. She shrugged her shoulders indifferently, disdainfully, and then, getting up, left the room with that light footstep of hers which scarcely seems to touch the earth.

"Cesare Dias smiled without looking at mc, and his smile disconcerted me horribly, putting all my thoughts into confusion. But I felt that I ought to make the attempt—I ought. I had promised it to you, my darling, and to myself. My life had become insupportable; the more so because of my sister, who knew my secret, who tortured me with her contempt—the contempt of a person who has never loved for one who does—who might at any moment betray me, and tell the story of that wintry night.

"Cesare Dias smiled, and didn't seem to care in the least to hear what I had to say. However, in spite of my emotion, in spite of the fact that I was talking to a man who cared nothing for me and for whom I cared nothing, in spite of the gulf that divides a character like mine from that of Cesare Dias, I had the courage to tell him that I adored you, that I wished to live and die with you, that my fortune would suffice for our needs, that I would never marry any one but you; and finally, that, humbly, earnestly, I besought him, as my guardian, my nearest relation, my wisest friend, to give his consent to our marriage.

"He had listened, with his eyes cast down, giving no sign of interest. And now at the end he simply uttered a dry little 'No.'

"And then took place a dreadful scene. I implored, I wept, I rebelled, I declared that my heart was free, that my person was free; and always I found that I was addressing a man of stone, hard and dry, with a will of iron, an utterly false point of view, a conventional standard based upon the opinion of the world, and a total lack of good feeling. Cesare Dias denied that I loved you, denied that you loved me, denied that any such thing as real love could exist—real love for which people live and die! He denied that love was a thing not to be forgotten; denied that love is the only thing that makes life worth while. His one word was No—no, no, no, from the beginning to the end of our talk. He made the most specious, extravagant, and cynical arguments to convince me that I was deceiving myself, that we were deceiving ourselves, and that it was his duty to oppose himself to our folly. Oh, how I wept! How I abased my spirit before that man, who reasoned in this cold strain! and how it hurts me now to think of the way I humiliated myself! I remember that while my love for you, dearest, was breaking out in wild utterance, I saw that he was looking admiringly at me, as in a theatre he might admire an actor who was cleverly feigning passion. He did not believe me; and two or three times my anger rose to such a point that I stooped to threaten him; I threatened to make a public scandal.

"'The scandal will fall on the person who makes it,' he said severely, getting up, to cut short the conversation.

"He went away. In the drawing-room I heard him talking quietly with Laura, as if nothing had happened, as if he hadn't left me broken-hearted, as if he didn't know that I was on my knees, in despair, calling upon the names of the Madonna and the Saints for help. But that man has no soul; and I am surrounded by people who think me a mad enthusiast.

"My love, my darling love, my constant thought—it is then decided: we must fly. We must fly. Here, like this, I should die. Anything will be better than this house; it is a prison. Anything is better than the galleys.

"I know that what I propose is very grave. According to the common judgment of mankind a young girl who elopes is everlastingly dishonoured. In spite of the sanctity of marriage, suspicion never leaves her. I know that I am throwing away a great deal for a dream of love. But that is my strange and cruel destiny—the destiny which has given me a fortune and taken away my father; given me a heart eager for affection and cut me off from all affection; given me the dearest and at the same time the least loving sister!

"For whom ought I to sacrifice myself, since those who loved me are dead, and those who live with me do not love me? I need love; I have found it; I will attach myself to it; I will not let it go. Who will weep for me here? No one. Whose hands will be stretched out to call me back? No one's. What memories will I carry away with me? None. I am lonely and misunderstood; I am flying from ice and snow to the warm sunlight of love. You are the sun, you are my love. Don't think ill of me. I am not like other girls, girls who have a home, a family, a nest. I am a poor pilgrim, seeking a home, a family, a nest. I will be your wife, your sweetheart, your servant; I love you. A life passed in the holy atmosphere of your love will be an absolution for this fault that I am committing. I know, the world will not forgive me. But I despise people who can't understand one's sacrificing everything for love. And those who do not understand it will pity me. I shall care for nothing but your love; you will forgive me because you love me.

"So, it is decided. On the third day after you receive this letter—that is, on Friday—leave your house as if you were going for a walk, without luggage, and take a cab to the railway station. Take the train that leaves Naples for Salerno at one o'clock, and arrives at Pompeii at two. I shan't be at the station at Pompeii—that might arouse suspicions; but I shall be in the streets of the dead city, looking at the ruins. Find me there—come as swiftly as you can—to the Street of Tombs, leading to the Villa of Diomedes, near to the grave of Nevoleia Tyche, 'a sweet Pompeiian child,' according to her epitaph. We will meet there, and then we will leave for Metaponto or Brindisi, and sail for the East. I have money. You know, Cesare Dias, to save himself trouble, has allowed me to receive my entire income for the past two years. Afterwards—when this money is spent—well, we will work for our living until I come of age.

"You understand? You needn't worry about me. I shall get out of the house, go to the station, and arrive at Pompeii without being surprised. I have a bold and simple plan, which I can't explain to you. It would not do for us to meet here in town, the risk would be too great. But leaving for Pompeii by separate trains, how can any one suspect us? Does my clearness of mind astonish you? My calmness, my precision? For twenty days I have been thinking of this matter; I have lain awake at night studying it in detail.

"Remember, remember: Friday, at noon, leave your house. At one, leave the station. At half-past two come to me at the grave of Nevoleia Tyche. Don't forget, for mercy's sake. If you shouldn't arrive at the right time, what would become of me, alone, at Pompeii, in anguish, devoured by anxiety?

"My sweetest love, this is the last letter you will receive from me. Why, as I write these words, does a feeling of sorrow come upon me, making me bow my head? The word *last* is always sad, whenever it is spoken. Will you always love me, even though far from your country, even though poor, even though unhappy? You won't accuse me of having wronged you? You will protect me and sustain me with your love? You will be kind, honest, loyal. You will be all that I care for in the world.

"This is my last letter, it is true, but soon now our wondrous future will begin—our life together. Remember, remember where I shall wait for you.

"ANNA."

Alone in his little house, Giustino Morelli read Anna's letter twice through, slowly, slowly. Then his head fell upon his breast. He felt that he was lost, ruined; that Anna was lost and ruined.

At that early morning hour the Church of Santa Chiara, white with stucco, rich with gold ornamentation, with softly carved marbles and old pictures, was almost empty. A few pious old women moved vaguely here and there, wrapped in black shawls; a few knelt praying before the altar. Anna Acquaviva and her governess, Stella Martini, were seated in the middle of the church, with their eyes bent on their prayer-books. Stella Martini had a worn, sunken face, that must have once been delicately pretty, with that sort of prettiness which fades before thirty. Anna wore a dark serge frock, with a jacket in the English fashion; and her black hair was held in place by a comb of yellow tortoise-shell. The warm pallor of her face was broken by no trace of colour. Every now and then she bit her lips nervously. She had held her prayer-book open for a long while without turning a page. But Stella Martini had not noticed this; she was praying fervently.

Presently the young girl rose.

"I am going to confession," she said, standing still, holding on to the back of her chair.

The governess did not seek to detain her. With a light step she crossed the church and entered a confessional.

There the good priest, with the round, childlike face and the crown of snow-white hair, asked his usual questions quietly, not surprised by the tremor in the voice that answered him. He knew the character of his penitent.

But Anna answered incoherently; often not understanding the sense of the simple words the priest addressed to her. Sometimes she did not answer at all, but only sighed behind the grating.

At last her confessor asked with some anxiety: "What is it that troubles you?"

"Father, I am in great danger," she said in a low voice.

But when he sought to learn what her danger was she would give him no details. He begged her to speak frankly, to tell him everything; she only murmured:

"Father, I am threatened with disgrace."

Then he became severe, reminding her that it was a great sin to come thus and trifle with a sacrament of the church, to come to the confessional and refuse to confess. He could not give her absolution.

"I will come another time," she said rising.

But now, instead of returning to her governess, who was still praying with her eyes cast down, Anna stole swiftly out of the church into the street, where she hailed a cab, and bade the cabman drive to the railway station. She drew down the blinds of the carriage windows, and there in the darkness she could scarcely suppress a cry of mingled joy and pain to find herself at last alone and free.

The cab rolled on and on; it was like the movement of a dream. The only thing she could think of was this beautiful and terrible idea, that she, Anna Acquaviva, had abandoned for ever her home and her family, carrying away only so much of her fortune as the purse in her pocket could hold, to throw herself into the arms of Giustino Morelli. No feeling of fear held her back. Her entire past life was ended, she could never take it up again; it was over, it was over.

In that sort of somnambulism which accompanies a decisive action, she was as exact and rigid in everything she had to do as an automaton. At the station she paid her cabman, and mechanically asked for a ticket to Pompeii at the booking-office.

"Single or return?" inquired the clerk.

"Single," she answered.

As almost every one who went to Pompeii took a return ticket, the clerk thought he had to do with an Englishwoman or an impassioned antiquary.

She put the ticket into the opening of her glove, and went into the first-class waiting-room. She looked about her quite indifferently, as if it was impossible that Cesare Dias or indeed any one of her acquaintance should see her there. She was conscious of nothing save a great need to go on, to go on; nothing else. It was the first time in her life that she had been out alone like this, yet she felt no surprise. It seemed to her that she had been travelling alone for years; that Cesare Dias, Laura Acquaviva, and Stella Martini were pale shadows of an infinitely distant past, a past anterior to her present existence; that they were people she had known in another world. She kept repeating to herself, like a child trying to remember a word,

"Pompeii, Pompeii, Pompeii."

But when she was climbing into the first-class compartment of the train, it seemed suddenly as if a force held her back, as if a mysterious hand forbade her going on. She trembled, and had to make a violent effort to enter the carriage, as if to brush aside an invisible obstacle. And, from that moment, a voice within her seemed to be murmuring confusedly to her conscience, warning her of the great moral crisis she was approaching; while before her eyes the blue Neapolitan coast was passing rapidly, where the wintry cold had given way to a warm scirocco. On, on, the morning train hurried her, over the land, by the sea, between the white houses of Portici, the pink houses of Torre del Greco, the houses, pink, white, and yellow, of Torre Annunziata—on, on. And Anna, motionless in her corner, gazing out of the window, beheld a vague, delicious vision of flowers and stars and kisses and caresses; and an icy terror, a sense of imminent peril, lay upon her heart. Oh, yes! In a brilliant vision she saw a future of love, of passion and tenderness, a fire-hued vision of all that soul and body could desire; yet constantly that still, small voice kept whispering to her conscience: "Don't go, don't go. If you go, you are lost."

And this presently became so unbearable that, when the train entered the brown, burnt-up country at the foot of Vesuvius, the country that surrounds the great ruin of Pompeii, despair was making her twist the handle of her purse violently with her fingers. The green vines and the laughing villages had disappeared from the landscape; the blue sea, with its dancing white waves, had disappeared; she was crossing a wide, desolate plain; and the volcano, with its eternal wreath of smoke, rose before her. And also had disappeared for ever the phantasms of her happiness! Anna was travelling alone, through a sterile land, where fire had passed, devastating all life, killing the flowers, destroying the people, their homes, their pleasures, their loves. And the voice within her cried: "This is a symbol of Passion, which destroys all things, and then dies itself."

And then she thought that she had chosen ominously in coming to Pompeii—a city of love, destroyed by fire, an everlasting reminder to those who saw it of the tragedy of life—Pompeii, with its hard heart of lava!

She descended from the carriage when the train stopped, and followed a family of Germans and two English clergymen out of the tiny station.

She went on, looking neither to right nor left, up the narrow, dusty lane that leads from the railway to the inn at the city's gate. Neither the Germans nor the clergymen noticed her; the solitary young woman, with the warm, pale face, and the great brown-black eyes that gazed straight forward, without interest in what they saw, the eyes of a soul consumed by an emotion. When they had all entered the house, she ensconced herself in a corner near a window, and looked out upon the path she had followed, as if waiting for somebody, or as if wishing to turn back.

And Anna was praying for the safe coming of Giustino. If she could but see him, if she could but hear his voice, all her doubts, all her pains, would fly away.

"I adore him! I adore him!" she thought, and tried thus to find strength with which to combat her conscience. Her heart was filled with a single wish—to see Giustino; he would give her strength; he was the reason for her life—he and love. She looked at her little child's watch, the only jewel she had brought away; she had a long time still to wait before two o'clock.

An old guide approached her, and offered to show her the ruins. She followed him mechanically. They traversed the Street of Hope, the Street of Fortune, where there are the deep marks of carriage wheels in the stone pavement; they entered houses and shops and squares; she looked at everything with vacant eyes. Twice the guide said: "Now let us visit the Street of Tombs and the Villa of Diomedes." Twice she had answered: "Later on; by-and-by."

Two or three times she had sat down on a stone to rest; and then her poor old guide had sat down also, at a distance, and let his head fall forward on his breast, and dozed. She was strangely fatigued; she had exhausted her forces in making the journey hither; the tumult of emotion she had gone through had prostrated her. Now she felt utterly alone and abandoned—a poor, unfortunate creature bearing through this dead city a heavy burden of solitude and weariness: and when, after a long rest, she got up to go on again, a great sigh broke from her lips.

But somehow she must pass the time, and so she went on. She climbed to the top of the Amphitheatre, seeking to devour the minutes that separated her from two o'clock.

Presently the old man said, for the third time: "Now let us visit the Street of Tombs and the Villa of Diomedes."

"Let us go," she responded.

The hours had passed at last; only one more remained. With her watch in her hand, as the guide pointed out to her the magnificence of the Villa of Diomedes, she was saying to herself, "Now Giustino is leaving Naples."

Impatient, no longer able to endure the voice or presence of the old man, no longer able to hide her own perturbation, she paid and dismissed him. He hesitated, reluctant to leave her, telling her that it was forbidden to make sketches, and, above all, to carry anything away; but he said it timidly, humbly, knowing very well that it was needless to fear any such infractions from this pale girl with the dreamy eyes. And he moved off, slowly, slowly, turning back every now and then to see what she was doing. She sat down on a stone in front of the tomb of the "sweet freed-woman," Nevoleia Tyche, and waited there, her hands in her lap, her head bent; nor did she look up when a party of English passed her, accompanied by a guide. This last hour seemed interminable to her; it seemed covered by a great shadow, in which all things were obscured. The name of Giustino, constantly repeated, was like a single ray of light. She neither heard nor saw what was going on round about her; her consciousness of the external world was put out.

Suddenly a shadow fell between her and the grey tomb of the freed-woman. She looked up, and saw Giustino standing before her, gazing down on her with an infinite despairing tenderness.

Anna, unable to speak, gave him her hand, and rose. And a smile of happiness, like a great light, shone from her eyes, and a warm colour mantled her cheeks. Giustino had never seen her so beautiful. In an ecstasy of joy, feeling all her doubts die within her, feeling all the glory of her love spring to full life again, Anna could not understand why there was an expression of sorrow on Giustino's face.

"Do you love me—a great deal?"

"A great deal."

"You will always care for me?"

"Always."

It was like a sad, soft echo, but the girl did not notice that; a veil of passion dimmed her perceptions. They walked on together, she close to him, so happy that her feet scarcely touched the earth, enjoying this minute of intense love with all the force of feeling that she possessed, with all the self-surrender of which human nature is capable. They walked on through the streets of Pompeii, without seeing, without looking. Only again and again she said softly: "Tell me that you love me—tell mc that you love me!"

Two or three times he had answered simply, "Yes," then he was silent.

Suddenly, Anna, not hearing his answer, stood still, and taking his arms in her hands, looked deep into his honest eyes, and asked, "What is the matter?"

Her voice trembled. He lowered his eyes.

"Nothing," he said.

"Why are you so sad?"

"I'm not sad," he answered with an effort.

"You're telling the truth?"

"I'm telling the truth."

"Swear that you love me."

"Do you need me to swear it?" he exclaimed with such sincerity and such pain that she was convinced, perceiving the sincerity, but not the pain.

But she was still troubled; there was still a bitterness in her joy. They were near the Street of the Sea, which leads out of the dead city.

"Let us go away, let us go away," she said impatiently.

"The train for Metaponto doesn't leave till six o'clock; we've plenty of time."

"Let us go away! I don't want to stay here any longer. I beg of you, let us go."

He obeyed her passively and was silent. They entered the inn on their way to the station, at the same time as the two English clergymen. Anna was frightened; she didn't care to talk of love to Giustino before such witnesses, but she looked at him with fond, supplicating eyes. The two clergymen seated themselves at the table which is always laid in the chief room of the inn, and while they ate their dinner one of them read his Bible, the other his Baedeker. The two lovers were near the window, looking through the glass at the road that leads to the station; and Anna was holding on to Giustino's arm, and he, confused, nervous, asked her if she would not like to dine, taking refuge from his embarrassment in the commonplace. "No; she did not wish to dine, she wasn't hungry. Afterwards, by-and-by." And her voice failed her as she looked at the two ecclesiastics.

"I wish——" she began, whispering into Giustino's ear.

"What do you wish?"

"Take me away somewhere else, where I can say something to you."

He hesitated; she blushed; then he left the room to speak to the landlord; returning presently, "Come," he said.

"Where are we going?"

"Upstairs."

"Upstairs?"

"You will see."

They went upstairs to the first floor, where the waiter who conducted them opened the door of an apartment consisting of a bedroom and sitting-room—a big bedroom, a tiny sitting-room—both having balconies that looked off over the country, and there the waiter left them alone.

Each of them was pale, silent, confused.

She looked round. The sitting-room was vulgarly furnished with a green sofa, two green easy-chairs, a centre-table covered with a nut-coloured jute tablecloth, and a marble console. The thought of the many strangers who had inhabited it inspired her with a sort of shame. Then she glanced into the bedroom. It was very large, with two beds at the farther end, a dressing-table, a sofa, and a wardrobe. These pieces of furniture seemed lost in the vast bare-looking chamber. It gave her a shudder merely to look into it; and yet again she blushed.

She raised her eyes to Giustino's, and she noticed anew that he was gazing at her with an expression of great sadness.

"What is the matter?" she asked.

He did not answer. He sat down and buried his face in his hands.

"Tell me what it is," she insisted, trembling with anger and anguish.

He remained silent. Perhaps he was weeping behind his hands.

"If you don't tell me what it is, I'll go back to Naples," she said.

He did not speak.

"You despise me because I have left my home."

"No, Anna," he murmured.

"You think I'm dreadful—you think of me as an abandoned creature."

"No, dear one—no."

"Perhaps—you—love another woman."

"You can't think that."

"Perhaps—you have—another tie—without love."

"None; I am bound to no one."

"You have promised yourself to no one?"

"To no one."

"Then why are you so sad? Why do you weep? Why do you tremble? It is I who ought to weep and tremble, and yet I don't weep unless to see you weep. Your weeping breaks my heart, makes me desperate."

"Anna, listen to me. By the memory of your mother I implore you to listen, to understand. I am miserable because of you, on your account—in thinking of what I have allowed you to do, of how you are throwing away your future, of the unhappiness that awaits you; without a home, without a name, persecuted by your family——"

"If you loved me, you wouldn't think these things; you wouldn't say them."

"I have always said them, Anna; I have always repeated them. I have ruined you. For three days I have been in an agony of remorse; it is the same to-day. Though you are the light of my life, I must say it to you. To-day I can't forgive myself; to-morrow you will be unable to forgive me. Oh, my love! I am a gentleman, I am a Christian; and yet I have been weak enough to allow you and me to commit this sin, this fault."

Speaking thus, with an infinite earnestness, all the honesty of his noble soul showed itself, a soul bowed down by remorse. She looked at him and listened to him with stupefaction, amazed at this spectacle of a rectitude, of a virtue that was greater than love, for she believed only in love.

"I don't understand you," she said.

"And yet you must—you must. If you don't see the reasons for my conduct you will despise me, you will hate me. You must try, with all your heart, with all your mind, to understand. You mustn't let yourself be carried away by your love. You must be calm, you must be cool."

"I can't."

"O God!" he said in despair.

Again he was silent. She mechanically, to overcome the trembling of her hands, pulled at the fringe of the tablecloth. She tried to reflect, to understand. And always, always, she had the same feeling, the same idea, and she could not help trying to express it in words: "You don't love me enough." She looked into his eyes as she spoke, concentrating her whole soul in her voice and in her gaze.

"It is true, I don't love you enough," he answered.

She made no sound: she was cut to the heart. The little sitting-room, the inn, Pompeii, the whole world appeared to go whirling round her dizzily. She had a feeling as if her temples would burst open, and pressed her hands to them instinctively.

"Ah, then," she said, after a long pause, in a broken voice—"ah, then, you have deceived me?"

"I have deceived you," he murmured humbly.

"You haven't loved me?"

"Not enough to forget everything else. I have already said so."

"I understand. What was the use of lying?"

"Because you were beautiful and good, and you loved me, and I didn't see this danger. I didn't dream that you would wish to give up everything in this way, that I should be unable to prevent you——"

"Words, words. The essential is, you don't love me."

"As you wish to be loved, as you deserve to be loved—no."

"That is, without blind passion?"

"Without blind passion."

"That is, without fire, without enthusiasm?"

"Without fire, without enthusiasm."

"Then, with what?"

"With tenderness, with affection, with devotion."

"It is not enough, not enough, not enough," she said monotonously, as if talking in her sleep. "Don't you know how to love differently. More—as I love——?"

"No, I don't know how."

"Do you think you never can? Perhaps you can to-morrow, or in the future?"

"No, I never can, Anna. I shall always prefer duty to happiness."

"Poor, weak creature," she murmured with immense scorn.

He lifted his eyes towards heaven, as if seeking strength to endure his martyrdom.

"So," Anna went on, slowly, "if we were to live together, you would be unhappy?"

"We should both be unhappy, and the sight of your unhappiness, of which I should be the cause, would kill me."

"Well, then?"

"It's for you to say what you wish."

The cruel, the terrible reality was clear to her; there was only one thing to be said, and that was so unexpectedly dreadful that she hesitated to say it. The truth was so horrible, she could not bear to give it shape in speech. She looked at him—at this man who, to save her, inflicted such inexpressible pain upon her. And he understood that Anna could not pronounce the last words. He himself, in spite of his great courage, could not speak them, those last words, for he loved the girl wildly. The terrible truth appalled them both.

She got up stiffly and went to the window and leaned her forehead against the glass, looking out over the country and down the lane that led to the little station. Twice before that day she had looked at the same silent landscape; but in the morning, when she was alone, waiting, thrilling with hope, and again, only an hour ago, leaning on Giustino's arm, she had possessed entire the priceless treasure of a great love. Now, now all was over; nevermore, nevermore would she know the delight of love: all was over, all, all.

Giustino had not moved from where he sat with his face buried in his hands. Suddenly Anna seized him by the shoulders, forced him to raise his head, and began to speak, so close to him that he could feel her warm breath on his cheek.

"And yet you did love me," she said, passionately. "You can't deny it; I know it. I have seen you turn pale when you met me, as pale as I myself. If I spoke to you my voice made your eyes brighten, as your voice made my heart leap. You looked for me everywhere, as I looked for you, feeling that the world would be colourless without love. And your letters bore the imprint of a great tenderness. But that is love, true love, passionate love, which isn't forgotten in a day or in a year, for which a whole life-time is not sufficient. It isn't possible that you don't love me any more. You do love me; you are deceiving me when you say you don't. I don't know why. But speak the truth—tell me that it is impossible for you to have got over such a passion."

He felt all his courage leaving him under this tumult of words.

"Giustino, Giustino, think of what you are doing in denying our love. Think of the two lives you are ruining; for you yourself will be as miserable as I. Giustino, you will kill me; if you leave me here, I shall kill myself. Let us go away; let us go away together. Take me away. You love me. Let us start at once; now is the time."

It seemed for a moment as if he were on the point of giving way. He was a man with a man's nerves, a man's senses, a man's heart; and he loved her ardently. But when again she begged him to fly with her, and he felt himself almost yielding, he made a great effort to resist her.

"I can't, Anna; I cannot," he said in a low voice.

"Then you wish me to die?"

"You won't die. You are young. You will live to be happy again."

"All is over for me, Giustino. This is death."

"No, it's not death, Anna."

"You talk like Cesare Dias," she cried, moving away from him. "You speak like a sceptic who has neither love nor faith. You are like him—corrupt, cynical——"

"You insult me; but you're right."

"I am dishonoured: do you realise that? I am a fugitive from my people; I am alone here with you in an hotel. I am dishonoured, dishonoured, coward that you are. You can go home quietly, having had an amusing adventure; but I—I have no home any more. I was a good girl; now I am lost."

"Your people know where you are and what you have done—that you have done nothing wrong. They know that you have done it in response to a generous impulse for one who was not worthy of you, but who has respected you."

"And who told them?"

"I."

"When?"

"This morning."

"To whom did you tell it?"

"To your sister and your guardian."

"Did they come to ask you?"

"No, I went to them."

"And what did you agree upon amongst you?"

"That I should come here and meet you."

"And then?"

"That I should leave you."

"When?"

"When Cesare Dias was ready to come and fetch you."

"It's a beautiful plan," she said, icily. "The plan of calm, practical men. Bravo, bravo! You—you ran to my people, to exculpate yourself, to accuse me, to reassure them. Good, good! I am a mad child, guilty of a youthful escapade, which fortunately hasn't touched my reputation. You denounced me, told them that I wanted to elope with you; and you are a gentleman! Good! The whole thing was wonderfully well combined. I am to return home with Cesare Dias as if I had made a harmless little excursion, and what's done is done. You're right, of course; Cesare Dias is right; Laura Acquaviva, who has never loved and who despises those who love, Laura is right; you are all right. I alone am wrong. Oh, the laughable adventure! To attempt an elopement, and to fail in it, because the man won't elope. To return home because your lover has denounced you to your family! What a comedy! You are right. There has been no catastrophe. The solution is immensely humorous: I know it. I am like a suicide who didn't kill herself. You are right. I am wrong. You—you——" And she looked him full in the face, withering him with her glance. "Begone! I despise you. Begone!"

"Anna, Anna, don't send me away like this."

"Begone! The cowardly way in which you have behaved is past contempt. Begone!"

"We mustn't part like this."

"We are already parted, utterly separated. We have always been separated. Go away."

"Anna, what I have done I have done for your sake, for your good. Now you send me away. Afterwards you will do me justice. I am an honourable man—that is my sin."

"I don't know you. Good-day."

"But what will you do alone here?"

"That doesn't concern you. Good-day."

"Let me wait for Cesare Dias."

"If you don't go at once I'll open the window and throw myself from the balcony," she said, with so much firmness that he believed her.

"Good-bye, then."

"Good-bye."

She stood in the middle of the room, a small red spot burning in each of her cheeks, and watched him go out, heard him descend the staircase, slowly, with the heavy step of one bearing a great burden. She leaned from the window and saw the shadow of a man issue from the door of the inn—it was Giustino. He stood still for a moment, and then turned into the high road that leads to Pompeii from Torre Annunziata, and again stood still, as if to wait for somebody there. Anna saw him turn towards the windows of the hotel, and gaze up at them earnestly. At last he moved slowly away and disappeared.

Anna came back into the room, and threw herself upon the sofa, biting its cushions to keep herself from screaming. Her head was on fire, but she couldn't weep—not a tear, not a single tear.

And in the midst of her trouble, constantly—whether, as at one moment, she was pitying herself as a poor child to whom a monstrous wrong had been done, or as, at the next, burning with scorn as a great lady offended in her pride; or again, blushing with shame as she thought of the imminent arrival of Cesare Dias—in the midst of it all, through it all, constantly, one little agonising, implacable phrase kept repeating itself: "All is over, all is over, all is over!"

Presently a servant brought in a light.

"Please, madam, do you mean to stay the night?" he asked.

"No."

"The last train for Naples has already left. You can go back by way of Torre Annunziata in a carriage."

"Some one is coming for me," she said.

The servant left the room.

By-and-by she heard her name called: "Anna! Anna!"

She fell on her knees before Cesare Dias, sobbing: "Forgive me, forgive me."

He, with a tremor in his voice, murmured, "My poor child."

And at home, in her own house, she said to her sister: "Laura, forgive me."

"My poor Anna."

III.

For three weeks Anna lay at the point of death, prey to a violent attack of scarlet fever, alternating between delirium and stupor, and always moaning in her pain; while Laura, Stella Martini, and a Sister of Charity watched at her bedside.

But she did not die. The fever reached its crisis, and then, little by little, day by day, abated.

At last her struggle with death was finished, but Anna had lost in it the best part of her youth. Thus a valorous warrior survives the battle indeed, but returns to his friends the phantom of himself—an object of pity to those who saw him set forth, strong and gallant.

When the early Neapolitan spring began to show itself, at the end of February, she was convalescent, but so weak that she could scarcely support the weight of her thick black hair. Stella Martini tried very patiently to comb it so gently that Anna should not have to move, braiding it in two long plaits; in this way it would seem less heavy. From time to time a big tear would roll down the invalid's cheek.

She was weeping silently, slowly; and when Laura or Stella Martini, or Sister Crocifissa would ask her: "What is it; what can we do for you?" Anna would answer with a sign which seemed to say: "Let me weep; perhaps it will do me good to weep."

"Let her weep, it will do her good to weep," was what the great doctor Antonio Amati had said also. "Let her do whatever pleases her; refuse her nothing if you can help it."

So her nurses, obedient to the doctor, did not try to prevent her weeping, did not even try to speak comforting words to her. Perhaps it was not so much an active sorrow that made her shed these tears, as a sort of sad relief.

Cesare Dias during this anxious time put aside his occupations of a gay bachelor, and called two or three times a day at the palace in Piazza Gerolomini to inquire how Anna was. The two girls had no nearer relative than he; and he, indeed, was not a relative: he was their guardian, an old friend of their father's, a companion of the youthful sports of Francesco Acquaviva. The young wife of Francesco had died five years after the birth of her second daughter, Laura, who resembled her closely: and thereupon her husband had proceeded to shorten his own life by throwing himself into every form of worldly dissipation. The two children, growing up in the house, motherless in the midst of profuse luxury, could exert no restraining influence upon their father, who seemed bent upon enjoying every minute of his existence as if he realised that its end was near. His constant companion was the cold, calm, sceptical Cesare Dias, a man who appeared to despise the very pleasures it was his one business to pursue. And when Francesco Acquaviva fell ill, and was about to die, he could think of nothing better than to make the partner of his follies the guardian of his children.

Cesare Dias had discharged his duties, not without some secret annoyance, with a gentlemanlike correctness; never treating his wards with much familiarity, rarely showing himself in public with them, keeping them at a distance, indeed, and feeling very little interest in them. He was their guardian—he, a man who, of all things, had least desired to have a family, who spent the whole of his income upon himself, who hated sentiment, who had no ideal of friendship. Cesare Dias, a man without tenderness, without affection, without sympathy, was the guardian of two young girls. He was this by the freak of Francesco Acquaviva. Dias would be glad enough when the day came for the girls to marry. When people congratulated him upon his situation as a rich bachelor with no obligations, he responded with a somewhat sarcastic smile: "Pity me rather; I've got two children—a legacy from Francesco Acquaviva."

"Oh, they'll soon be married."

"I hope so," he murmured devoutly.

As he watched the girls grow up, the character of Laura, haughty, and reserved, and silent, as if she had already known a thousand disillusions, began vaguely to please him, as if he saw obscurely in a looking-glass a face that distantly resembled his own: a faint admiration which was really but reflex admiration of himself. The character of Anna, on the contrary, open, loyal, impressionable and impulsive, a character full of strong likes and dislikes—imaginative, enthusiastic, generous—had always roused in him a certain antipathy.

In her presence he seemed even colder and more indifferent than elsewhere; merciless for all human weakness, disdainful of all human interests.

It would have been a miracle if two such incompatible natures, each so positive, had not repelled each other. Sometimes, though, Anna could not help feeling a certain secret respect for this man, who perhaps had good reasons—reasons born of suffering—for the contempt with which he regarded his fellow-beings; and sometimes Dias told himself that it was ridiculous to be angry with this strange child, for she was a worthy daughter of Francesco Acquaviva, a man who had tossed his life to the winds of pleasure. Dias asked himself scornfully, "What does it matter?"

And so, when he learned that his ward had fallen in love with an obscure and penniless youth, he shrugged his shoulders, murmuring, "Rhetoric!" He deemed it wiser not to speak to her about the matter, for he knew that the flame of love is only fanned by the wind of contradiction; besides, it is always useless to talk sensibly to a silly girl.

When Giustino Morelli had called upon him and humbly asked for Anna's hand, Dias opposed to the ingenuous eloquence of love the cynical philosophy of the world, and thought his trouble ended when he saw the young man go away, pale and resigned. "Rhetoric, rhetoric!" was his mental commentary; and he had a theory that what he called rhetoric could be trusted to die a natural death. So he went back to his usual occupation, giving the affair no further thought.

But chemical analysis cannot explain spontaneous generation; criticism cannot explain genius; and no more can cold reason explain or understand youthful passion.

When it came to the knowledge of Cesare Dias that Anna had left her home to give herself into the keeping of a poor nobody, he was for a moment stupefied; he seemed for a moment to have a vision of that force whose existence he had hitherto doubted, which can lift hearts up to dizzy heights, and human beings far above convention. He was a man of few words, a man of action, but now he was staggered, nonplussed. A child who could play her reputation and her future like this, inspired him with a sort of vague respect, a respect for the power that moved her. Ah, there was a convulsion in the soul of Cesare Dias, the man of fixed ideas and easy aphorisms, who suddenly found himself face to face with a moral crisis in which the life of his young ward might be wrecked. And he felt a pang of self-reproach. He ought to have watched more carefully over her; he ought to have been kinder to her; he ought not to have left her to walk unguided in the dangerous path of youth and love.

He felt a certain pity for the poor weak creature, who had gone, as it were, headlong over a precipice without calling for help. He thought that, if she had been his own daughter, he would have endeavoured to cultivate her common sense, to show her that it was impossible for people to live constantly at concert pitch. He had, therefore, failed in his duty towards her, in his office of protector and friend; and yet what faith her dead father, Francesco Acquaviva, had had in him, in his wisdom, in his affection! Anna, who had hitherto inspired him only with that disdain which practical men feel for sentimentalists, now moved him to compassion, as a defenceless being exposed to all the slings and arrows of outrageous fortune. And during his drive from Naples to Pompeii he promised himself that he would be very kind to her, very gentle. If she had flown from her home, it was doubtless because the love that Giustino Morelli bore her had appeared greater to her than the love of her own people; and doubtless, too, there are hearts to whom love is as necessary as bread is to the body. Never before had Cesare Dias felt such an emotion as beset him now during that long drive to Pompeii; for years he had been on his guard against such emotions.

And, accordingly, after that fatal day on which he brought her back to her house, he and Laura and Stella Martini all tried to create round Anna a peaceful atmosphere of kindness and indulgence, as if she had committed a grave but generous error, by whose consequences she alone was hurt. Laura—silent, thoughtful, with her dreamy grey eyes, her placid face—nursed Anna through her fever with quiet sisterly devotion. Cesare Dias called every morning, entering the room on tiptoe, inquiring with a glance how the sufferer was doing, then seating himself at a distance from the bed, without speaking. If Anna looked up, if he felt her big sorrowful black eyes turned upon his face, he would ask in a gentle voice, the voice of *that day*, how she felt; she would answer with a faint smile, "Better," and would shut her eyes again, and go back to her interior contemplations.

Cesare Dias, after that, would get up noiselessly and go away, to come again in the afternoon, and still again in the evening, perhaps for a longer visit.

Laura, always dressed in white, would meet him in the sitting-room; and he would ask, "Is she better?"

"She seems to be."

"Has she been asleep to-day?"

"No, I don't think she has been asleep."

"Has she said anything."

"Not a word."

"Who is to watch with her to-night."

"I."

"You will wear yourself out."

"No, no."

Nothing else passed between them.

Often he would arrive in the evening wearing his dress-suit; he had dined at his club, and was off for a card-party or a first night at a theatre. Then he would remain standing, with his overcoat open, his hat in his hand. At such a time, a little warmed up by the dinner he had eaten, or the amusements that awaited him, Cesare Dias was still a handsome man; his dull eyes shone with some of their forgotten brightness; his cheeks had a little colour in them; and his smooth black hair gave him almost an appearance of youth. One who had seen him in the morning, pale and exhausted, would scarcely have recognised him. Laura would meet him and part with him, never asking whence he came or whither he was bound; when he had said good-night she would return to Anna, slowly, with her light footsteps that merely brushed the carpet.

Cesare Dias told himself that if he wished to make his sick ward over morally, now was the time to begin, while her body was weak and her soul malleable. It would be impossible to transform her spirit after she had once got back her strength. Anna was completely prostrated, passing the entire day without moving, her arms stretched out at full length, her hands pale and cold, her face turned on the side, her two rich plaits of black hair extended on her pillow; bloodless her cheeks, her lips, her brow; lifeless the glance of her eyes. When spoken to, she answered with a slight movement of the head, or, at most, one or two words—always the same.

"How do you feel?"

"Better."

"Do you wish for anything?"

"Nothing."

"Is there nothing you would like?"

"No, thanks."

Whereupon she would close her eyes again, exhausted. Nothing more would be said by those round her, but Anna knew that they were there, silent, talking together by means of significant glances.

One day, Cesare Dias and Laura Acquaviva felt that they could mark a progress in Anna's convalescence, because two or three times she had looked at them with an expression of such earnest penitence, with such an eager prayer for pardon, in her sad dark eyes, that words were not necessary to tell what she felt. Soon afterwards she seemed to wish to be left alone with Dias, as if she had a secret to confide to him; but he cautiously thought it best to defer any private talk. However, one morning it so happened that he found himself alone in her room. He was reading a newspaper when a soft voice said:

"Listen."

Cesare Dias looked at her. Her black eyes were again beseeching forgiveness, and Anna stammered:

"What must you have thought—what must you have said of me!"

"You must not excite yourself, my dear," he said kindly.

"I was so wicked," she sobbed.

"Don't talk like that, dear Anna; you were guilty of nothing more than a girlish folly."

"A sin, a sin."

"You must call things by their right names, and not let your imagination get the better of you," he answered, somewhat coldly. "A youthful folly."

"Well, be it as you wish," she said, humbly; "but if you knew——"

"There, there," murmured Cesare Dias with the shadow of a smile, "calm yourself; we'll speak of this another day."

Laura had come back into the room, and her presence cut short their talk.

That evening, by the faint light of a little lamp that hung before an image of the Virgin at her bedside, Anna saw the big grey eyes of Laura gazing at her inquiringly; and therewith she raised herself a little on her pillow and called her sister to her.

"You are good; you don't know——"

"You mustn't excite yourself."

"You are innocent, Laura, but you are my sister. Don't judge me harshly."

"I don't judge you, Anna."

"Laura, Laura——"

"Be quiet, Anna."

Laura's tone was a little hard, but with her hand she gently caressed her sister's cheek; and Anna said nothing more.

As her recovery progressed, an expression of humility, of contrition, seemed to become more and more constant upon her face when she had to do with Laura or with Dias.

They were very kind to her, with that pitying kindness which we show to invalids, to old people, and to children—a kindness in marked contrast to their former indifference, which awoke in her an ever sharper and sharper remorse. She felt a great difference between herself and them: they were sane in body and mind, their blood flowed tranquilly in their veins, their consciences were untroubled; while she was broken in health, disturbed in spirit, and miserable in thinking of her past, its deceits, its errors, its thousand shameful aberrations, its lack of maidenly decorum—and for whom? for whom? For a fool, a simpleton, a fellow who had neither heart nor courage, who had never loved her, who was cruel and inept. When she drew a mental comparison between Giustino Morelli and these two persons whom she had wished to desert for him—between Giustino, so timid, so poor in all right feeling, so bankrupt in passion, and them, so magnanimous, so forgetful of her fault—her repentance grew apace. It was the exaggerated repentance of a noble nature, which magnifies the moral gravity of its own transgressions. She felt herself to be quite undeserving of the sympathy and affection with which they treated her. Their kindness was an act of gratuitous charity beyond her merits.

She would look from Laura to Cesare Dias and murmur: "You are good; you are good." And then at the sound of her own voice she would be so moved that she would weep; and pale, with great dark circles under her eyes, she would repeat, "So good, so good."

Her sole desire was to show herself absolutely obedient to whatever her guardian demanded, to whatever her sister advised.

She gave herself over, bound hand and foot, to these two beings whom she had so cruelly forgotten on the day of her mad adventure; in her convalescence she found a great joy in throwing herself absolutely upon their wisdom and their goodness.

Little by little it seemed to her that she was being born again to a new life, quiet, placid, irresponsible; a life in which she would have no will of her own, in which, passively, gladly, she would be guided and controlled by them. So, whenever they spoke to her, whenever they asked for her opinion—whether a window should be opened or closed, whether a bouquet of flowers should be left in the room or carried out, whether a note should be written to a friend who had called to inquire how she was—she always said, "Yes," or "As you think best," emphasising her answer with a gesture and a glance.

"Yes" to whatever Cesare Dias suggested to her; Cesare Dias who had grown in her imagination to the proportions of a superior being, far removed from human littleness, invincible, dwelling in the highest spheres of abstract intellect; and "Yes" to whatever Laura Acquaviva suggested, Laura the pure, the impeccable, who had never had the weakness to fall in love, who would die rather than be wanting to her ideal of herself. "Yes" even to whatever her poor governess, Stella Martini, suggested; Stella so kind, so faithful, whom in the past she had so heartlessly deceived. "Yes" to the good Sister of Charity, Maria del Crocifisso, who passed her life in self-sacrifice, in self-abnegation, in loving devotion to others. "Yes" to everybody. Anna said nothing but "Yes," because she had been wrong, and they had all been right.

She was getting well. Nothing remained of her illness except a mortal weakness, a heaviness of the head, an inability to concentrate her mind upon one idea, a desire to rest where she was, not to move from her bed, from her room, not to lift her hands, to keep her eyes closed, her cheek buried in her pillow. Cesare Dias called daily after luncheon, at two o'clock, an hour when men of the world have absolutely nothing to do, for visits are not in order till four. The girls waited for him every afternoon; Laura with her appearance of being above all earthly trifles, showing neither curiosity nor eagerness; Anna with a secret anxiety because he would bring her a sense of calmness and strength, a breath of the world's air, and especially because he seemed so firm, so imperturbable, that she found it restorative merely to look at him, as weaklings find restorative the sight of those who are robust. He would chat a little, giving the latest gossip, telling where last night's ball had been held, who had gone upon a journey, who had got married, but always with that tone of disdain, that tone of the superior being who sees but is not moved, and yet who seeks to conceal his boredom, which was characteristic of him.

Sometimes, though, he would laugh outright at the society he moved in, at its pleasures, at its people, burlesquing and caricaturing them, and ridiculing himself for being led by them.

"Oh, you!" cried Anna, with an indescribable intonation of respect.

She listened eagerly to everything he said. Her fragile soul was like a butterfly that lights on every tiniest flower. These elegant and meaningless frivolities, these experiences without depth or significance, these axioms of a social code that turned appearances into idols, all this worthless baggage delighted her enfeebled imagination. Her heart seemed to care for nothing but little things. She admired Cesare Dias as a splendid and austere man whom destiny had thrown amidst inferior surroundings, and who adapted himself to them without losing any of his nobler qualities. She told herself that his was a great soul that had been born too soon, perhaps too late; he was immeasurably above his times, yet with quiet fortitude he took them in good part. When he displayed his scorn for all human ambitions, speaking of how transitory everything pertaining to this world is in its nature; when he derided human folly and human beings who in the pursuit of follies lose their fortunes and their reputations; when he said that the only human thing deserving of respect was success; when he said that all generosity was born of some secret motive of selfishness, that all virtue was the result of some weakness of character or of temperament—she, immensely impressed, having forgotten during her fever the emotional reasons to be opposed to such effete and corrupt theories, bowed her head, answering sadly, "You are right."

Now that she was able to sit up they were often alone together. Laura would leave them to go and read in the sitting-room, or to receive callers in the drawing-room, or to walk out with Stella Martini. She could always find some pretext for taking herself off. She was a reserved, silent girl, who knew neither how to live nor how to love as others did. It was best to leave her to her taste for silence, for self-absorption. Cesare Dias, a little anxious about her, asked Anna:

"What is the matter with Laura?"

"She is good—she is the best girl alive," Anna answered, with the feeling she always showed when she named her sister.

Cesare Dias looked at her fixedly. He looked at her like this whenever her voice betrayed emotion. It seemed to him that it was her old nature revealing itself again; he wished to stamp it out, to suffocate it. Her heart was defenceless, too impressionable, the heart of a child: he wished to turn it into a heart of bronze, which would be unaffected by the breath of passion. Always, therefore, when Anna allowed her soul to vibrate in her voice, Cesare Dias, naturally serious and composed enough, seemed to become more serious, more austere; his eye hardened into glass, and Anna felt that she had displeased him. She knew that she displeased him as often as anything in her manner could recall that wild adventure which had sullied the innocence of her girlhood: as often as she gave any sign of being deeply moved: if she turned pale, if she bowed her head, if she wept. Cesare Dias hated all such manifestations of sentimental weakness. Sometimes, when Anna could no longer control herself, and her emotion could not be prevented from shining in her eyes, he would pretend not to notice it. Sometimes he would demand, "What is the matter?"

"Nothing," said she, timidly conscious that by her timidity she but displeased him the more.

"Always the same—incorrigible," he murmured, shaking his head hopelessly.

"Forgive me; I can't help it," she besought him with an imploring glance.

"You shouldn't say of anything that you can't help it. You should be strong enough to govern yourself in all circumstances," was the axiom of Cesare Dias.

"I will try."

One day in April, Stella Martini, coming home from a walk with Laura, brought her some flowers—some beautiful wild rosebuds, which in Naples blossom so early in the year. Anna was seated in an easy-chair near the window, through which entered the soft spring air; and when she saw Laura and Stella come into the house—Laura dressed in white, breathing peace and youth from every line of her figure—Stella with her face that seemed to have been scalded and shrivelled up by tears shed long ago, both bearing great quantities of fresh sweet roses, the poor girl's heart swelled with indescribable tenderness.

Holding the roses in her hand, she caressed them, touched them with her face, buried her lips in them, and said under her voice: "Thank you, thank you," as if in her weakness she could find no other words to express her pleasure.

Cesare Dias, arriving a little later, found her in rapt contemplation over her flowers, her great fond eyes glowing with joy. A shadow crossed his face.

"See, they have brought me these flowers," she said. "Aren't they lovely?"

"I see them," he said, drily.

"Aren't you fond of flowers? They're so fresh and fragrant. I hope you're fond of them; I adore them."

And in the fervour of her last phrase she closed her eyes.

It occurred to him that she had doubtless not so very long ago spoken the same words of a man; and he realised that, in spite of her illness, in spite of her repentance, she was ever the same Anna Acquaviva who had once flown from her home and people. He lifted his eyebrows, and his ebony walking-stick beat rather nervously against his chair.

"Would you like a rose?" she asked, to placate him.

"No."

"Why not?"

"Because I don't care for flowers."

"What! Not even to wear in your button-hole when you go into society?" she asked, trying to jest.

"They're not *de rigueur*. Flowers are pretty enough in their way; but I assure you I have never had the weakness to weep over them, or to say that I adore them."

"I was wrong, I said too much."

"You always say too much. You lack a sense of proportion. There are a great many things a girl shouldn't say, lest, if she begins by saying them, she should end by doing them, The woman who says too much is lost."

Anna turned as white as the collar of her frock. It had come at last, the reproof she had so long been waiting for, and secretly dreading. He had put it in a single brief sentence. The woman who says too much is lost. Once upon a time, six months ago for instance, she would have endured such a reproof from no one, such a bitter reference to her past; she would have retorted hotly, especially if the speaker had been Cesare Dias. But now! So weakened was she by her illness and her sorrow, there was not a fibre in her that resented it; her blood slept in her veins; her heart contained nothing but penitence. "The woman who says too much is lost!" Cesare Dias was right.

"It is true," she said.

And yet, as she said it, a new grief was born within her, as if she had renounced some precious possession of her soul, broken some holy vow.

Cesare's face cleared. He had won a victory.

"Anna," he went on, "every time that you allow yourself to be carried away by sentimentalism, that you employ exaggerated expressions, that you indulge in emotional rhetoric, I assure you, you displease me greatly. How ridiculous if life were to be passed in saying of people, houses, landscapes, flowers, 'I adore them!' Don't you see what a convulsive, hysterical frame of mind that is? As if life were nothing but a smile, a tear, a kiss! Do you know to what this sort of thing inevitably leads? You know——"

"Spare me, I entreat you."

"I can't, dear. First you must agree with me that your attitude towards life, though a generous one if you like, is not a wise one, and that it leads to the gravest errors. Am I right?"

"You are right."

"You must agree with me that that sort of thing can only make ourselves and others miserable, whereas our duty is to be as happy and to make others as happy as we can. Everything else is rhetoric. Am I right?"

"You are right. You are always right."

"Finally, you must agree that it is better to be reasonable than to be sentimental; better to be arid than to be rhetorical, better to be silent than to speak out everything that is in one's heart; better to be strong than to be weak. Am I not right?"

"You are right, always right."

"Anna, do you know what life is?"

"No, I don't know what it really is."

"Life is a thing which is serious and absurd at the same time."

She made no answer; she was silent and pensive.

"It is serious because it is the only thing we know anything about; because every man and every woman, in whatever rank or condition, is bound to be honest, well-behaved, worthy and proper; because if one is rich and noble it is one's duty to be moral in a given way; if one is poor and humble, it is one's duty to be moral in another way."

He saw that she was listening to him eagerly; he saw that he might hazard a great stroke.

"Giustino Morelli——" he began softly.

"No!" she cried, pressing her hands to her temples, her face convulsed with terror.

"Giustino Morelli——" he repeated calmly.

"For Heaven's sake, don't speak of him."

Cesare Dias appeared neither to see nor hear her. He wished to go to the bottom of the matter, courageously, pitilessly.

"—was a serious person, an honest man," he concluded.

"He was an infamous traitor," said Anna, in a low voice, as if speaking to herself.

"Anna, he was an honest man. You ought to believe it. You will believe it."

"Never, never."

"Yes, you will. You ought to do him justice. I, who am a man, I must do him justice. He might have issued from his obscurity; he might have had money, a beautiful wife, a wife whom he loved, for he loved you——"

"No, no."

"Everybody loves in his own way, my dear," retorted Cesare, icily. "He loved you. But because he did not wish to be thought self-interested, because he did not wish the world to say of him that he had loved you for your money, because he did not wish to hear you, Anna, some day say the same thing; because he could not endure the accusation of having seduced a young girl for her fortune; because he was not willing to let you suffer, as for some years, at any rate, you would have had to suffer, from poverty and obscurity, he renounced you. Do you understand? He renounced you because he was honest. He renounced you, though in doing so he had to face your anger and your scorn. My dear, that man was a martyr to duty, to use one of your own phrases. Will you allow me to say something which may appear ungracious, but which is really friendly?"

Anna consented with a sign.

"Well, you have no just notion of the seriousness of life. All its responsibilities can be scattered by a caprice, by a passion, to quote what you yourself have said. You would brush aside all obstacles; and you would run the risk of losing all respect, all honour, all peace, all health, thereby. Life, Anna, is a very serious affair."

With a bowed head, she could only answer by a gesture, a gesture that said "Yes."

"And, at the same time, it's a trifling matter, Anna."

It was the corrupt, effete nobleman who now re-appeared, the *viveur* who had drunk at every fountain, who was always bored and always curious; it was he who now took the place of the moral teacher. Anna looked up, surprised and shocked.

"Life is absurd, ridiculous, contemptible. The world is full of cruel parents, of false friends, of wives who betray their husbands, of husbands who maltreat their wives, of well-dressed swindlers, of thieving bankers. All of them in turn are judges and criminals. All appearances are deceitful; all faces lie. If by chance there turns up a man who seems really honest, nobody believes in him; or, if people believe in him, they despise him. The man who sacrifices himself, who makes some great renunciation—poor Morelli—gets nothing but disdain."

"But—if all this is true?" cried Anna sadly.

"Then, one must have the strength to keep one's own real feelings hidden; one must wear a mask; one must take other men and women at their proper value; one must march straight forward."

"Whether happy or miserable?"

She put this question with great anxiety, for she felt that when it was answered her soul's point of interrogation would be changed to a full stop.

"The strong are happy; the weak are miserable. Only the strong can triumph."

She was silent, oppressed and pained by his philosophy, by its bitterness, its sterile pride, its egotism and cruelty. It seemed as if he had built a sepulchre from the ruins of her illusions. She felt that she no longer understood either her own nature or the external world; a sense of fear and of confusion had taken the place of her old principles and aspirations. And there was a great home-sickness in her heart for love, for devotion, for tenderness, for enthusiasm; a great melancholy at the thought that she would never thrill with them again, that she would never weep again. She felt a great indefinable longing, not for the past, not for the present, not for the future, a longing that related itself to nothing. And she realised that what Cesare Dias had said was true—horribly, dreadfully, certainly true. She could be sure of nothing after this, she had lost her pole-star, she was being swept round and round in a spiritual whirlpool. And he who had led her into it inspired her with fear, respect, and a vague admiration. He himself had got beyond the whirlpool, he was safe in port. Perhaps, in despair, he had thrown overboard into the furious waves the most precious part of his cargo; perhaps he was little better than a wreck; but what did it matter? He was safe in harbour.

She was not sure whether it was better to brave out the tempest, to lose everything nobly and generously for the sake of love, or to save appearances, make for still waters, and in them enjoy a selfish tranquillity.

"You are strong?" she said.

"Yes," he assented.

"And are you happy—really?"

"Very happy. As happy as one can be."

By-and-by she asked: "Have you always been happy?"

Cesare Dias did not answer.

"Tell me, tell me, have you always been happy?"

"What does the past matter? Nothing."

"And—have you ever loved?"

"The person who says too much is lost; the person who wants to know too much suffers. Don't ask."

She chose a rose and offered it to him. He took it and put it into his button-hole.

At that instant Laura Acquaviva entered the room.

IV.

At the opening of the San Carlo theatre on Christmas night the opera was "The Huguenots."

A first night at the San Carlo is always an event for the Neapolitan public, no matter what opera, old or new, is given; but when the work happens to be a favourite the excitement becomes tremendous.

The two thousand persons, male and female, who constitute society in that town of half a million inhabitants, go about for a week beforehand, from house to house, from café to café, predicting that the evening will be a success. The chief rôles in "The Huguenots" were to be taken by De Giuli Borsi and Roberto Stagno, rôles in which the public was to hear these artists for the first time, though they were already known to everybody, either by reputation or from having been heard in other operas.

So, on that Christmas Day, the two thousand members of Neapolitan society put aside their usual occupations and arranged their time in such wise as to be ready promptly at eight o'clock, the men in their dress-suits, the women in rich and beautiful evening toilets. Everybody gave up something—a walk, a call, a luncheon, a nap—for the sake of getting betimes to the theatre.

By half-past seven the approaches to San Carlo, its portico, its big and little entrances, all brilliantly lighted by gas, were swarming like an ant-hill with eager people. Some came on foot, the collars of their overcoats turned up, showing freshly shaven faces under their tall silk opera-hats, or freshly waxed moustaches and beards newly pointed; others came in cabs; and before the central door, under the portico, which was draped with flags, passed a constant stream of private carriages, depositing ladies muffled in opera-cloaks of red velvet or white embroidery.

By a quarter past eight the house was full.

Anna and Laura Acquaviva, dressed in white silk, and accompanied by Stella Martini, occupied Box No. 19 of the second tier.

Cesare Dias had a place in Box No. 4 of the first tier.

Anna kept her eyes fixed upon him. He glanced up at her, but did not bow. He only turned and spoke a few words to the young man next to him, who thereupon aimed his opera-glass, at the girls' box; he was a young gentleman of medium height, with a blonde beard, and blonde hair brushed straight back from his forehead. His brown eyes had an expression of great kindness.

Anna kept her gaze fixed upon Cesare Dias; if now and then she turned it towards the stage it would only be for a brief moment.

"That is Luigi Caracciolo," said Laura.

"Who?" asked Anna.

"Luigi Caracciolo, the man next to Dias."

"Ah."

And again, Anna turned her face towards Box No. 4, where Cesare Dias sat with Luigi Caracciolo. The rest of the theatre hung round her in a sort of coloured mist; the only thing she clearly saw was the narrow space where those two men sat together.

Did they feel the magnetism of her gaze?

Cesare Dias, leaning forward, with his arm on the red velvet of the railing, was listening to the music of Meyerbeer; now and then he cast an absent-minded glance round the audience, the glance of a man who knows beforehand that he will find the usual people in the usual places.

Luigi Caracciolo appeared to give little heed to the music. He was pulling his blonde beard, and studying the ladies in the house through his opera-glass, while a slight smile played upon his lips. Presently he fixed his glass on Anna's box. Had he felt that magnetism? At any rate, he kept his glass fixed upon Anna's box.

The curtain fell on the first act.

Cesare Dias spoke a word or two to Luigi, and the two men rose and left their places.

Suddenly it seemed to Anna as if all the lights in the theatre had been put out.

"Stagno sang divinely," said Stella Martini.

"Yes," responded Laura. "But didn't it strike you that he rather exaggerated?"

"No, I can't say it did."

Anna did not hear; her eyes were closed.

There was a rumour in the house of moving people; there was a sound of opening and closing doors. Fans fluttered, men changed their seats, people went and came, many of the stalls were empty. The round of visits had begun. Husbands and brothers left their boxes to make place for other men beside their wives and sisters; to pay their respects to other men's wives and sisters. There was a babble of many voices idly chatting. It began in the first and second tiers, and it rose to the galleries, the stronghold of students, workmen, and clerks.

Anna gazed sadly at that deserted box below her.

All at once she heard Laura say, "Luigi Caracciolo and Cesare Dias are with the Contessa d'Alemagna."

Anna turned round, and raised her opera-glass.

They were there indeed, visiting the beautiful Countess; Anna could see the pale and noble face of Cesare Dias, the youthful face of Caracciolo. The Contessa d'Alemagna was an Austrian, very clever, very witty. She wore a costume of red silk, and kept waving a fan of red feathers, as she talked vivaciously with the two men. She must have been saying something extremely interesting, to judge by the close attention with which they listened to her and by the smiles with which they responded.

When Anna put down her opera-glass, her face had become deathly pale.

"Are you feeling ill?" asked Stella Martini.

"No," the child replied, paler than ever.

"Perhaps it's too hot here for you. Shall I open the door of the box?" suggested the governess.

"Laura, will you change seats with me?" said Anna.

Laura took Anna's place, and Anna retired to the back of the box, where she closed her eyes.

"Do you feel better, dear?"

"Thanks. Much better. It was the heat."

And she made as if to return to the front of the box, but Stella detained her, fearing that the heat there might again disturb her. So Anna stopped where she was, breathing the fresh air that came through the open door.

"Do you like 'The Huguenots,' Stella?" she asked, for the sake of saying something, in the hope, perhaps, of thus forgetting her desire to see what was going on in the box of the Contessa d'Alemagna.

"Very much. And you?"

"I like it immensely."

"I am afraid—I am afraid that later on you may find it too exciting. You know the fourth act is very terrible. Don't you dread the impression it may make upon you?"

"It won't matter, Stella," she said, with a faint smile.

"Perhaps you would like to go home before the fourth act begins. If you feel nervous about it——"

"I am not nervous," she murmured, as if speaking to herself. "Or, if I am, I'd rather suffer this way than otherwise."

"We were wrong to come," said Stella, shaking her head.

"No, no, Stella. Let us stay. I am all right; I am enjoying it. Don't take me home yet."

And she went back to the front of the box, to the seat next to Laura's.

"Cesare Dias and Luigi Caracciolo have left the Contessa d'Alemagna," said Laura.

"Already?"

"Perhaps they will come here," suggested Stella Martini.

"I don't think so. There won't be time," said Laura.

"There won't be time," assented Anna.

The house had become silent again, in anticipation of the second act. Here and there some one who had delayed too long in a box where he was visiting, would say good-bye quietly, and return to his place. A few such visitors, better acquainted with their hosts, remained seated, determined not to move. Among the latter were, of course, the lovers of the ladies, the intimate friends of the husbands.

From her present station Anna Acquaviva could not look so directly down upon Box No. 4 of the first tier as from her former; she had to turn round a little in order to see it, and thus her interest in it was made manifest. Cesare Dias and Luigi Caracciolo, after their visit to the Contessa d'Alemagna, had taken a turn in the corridor to smoke a cigarette, and had then returned to their places. Anna, the creature of her hopes and her desires, could not resist the temptation to gaze steadily at her guardian, though she felt that thereby she was drawing upon herself the attention of all observers, and exposing her deepest feelings to ridicule and misconstruction.

And now the divine music of Meyerbeer surged up and filled the hall, and Anna was conscious of nothing else—of nothing but the music and the face of Cesare Dias shining through it, like a star through the mist. How much time passed? She did not know. Twice her sister spoke to her; she neither heard nor answered.

When the curtain fell again, and Anna issued from her trance, Laura said, "There is Giustino Morelli."

"Ah!" cried Anna, unable to control a contraction of her features.

But she had self-constraint enough not to ask "*where?*" Falling suddenly from a heaven of rapture to the hard reality of her life, where traces of her old folly still lingered; hating her past, and wishing to obliterate it from her memory, as the motives for it were already obliterated from her heart, she did not ask where he was. She covered her face with her fan, and two big tears rolled slowly down her cheeks.

Stella Martini looked at her, desiring to speak, but fearing lest thereby she might only make matters worse.

At last: "We were wrong to come here, Anna," she said.

"No, no," responded Anna. "I am very well—I am very happy," she added, enigmatically.

The door of the box was slowly pushed open. Cesare Dias and Luigi Caracciolo entered. With a word or two their guardian presented the young man to the sisters. The men sat down, Cesare Dias next to Anna, Luigi Caracciolo next to Laura. They began at once to talk in a light vein about the performance. Overcoming the tumult of her heart, Anna alone answered them. Stella Martini was silent, and Laura, with her eyes half shut, listened without speaking.

"Stagno is a great artist; he is immensely talented," observed Luigi Caracciolo, with a bland smile, passing his fingers slowly through his blonde beard.

"And so much feeling—so much sentiment," added Anna.

"To say that he is talented, that he is an artist, is enough," replied Cesare Dias, with an accent in which severity was tempered by politeness.

Anna assented, bowing her head.

"For the rest, the number of decent opera singers on the modern stage is becoming less and less. We have a multitude of mediocrities, with here and there a star," continued Luigi Caracciolo.

"Ah, I have heard the great ones," sighed Cesare Dias.

"Yes, yes. You must have heard Fraschini, Negrini, and Nourrit in their time," Luigi Caracciolo said, smiling with the fatuity of a fellow of twenty who imagines that his youth will last for ever.

"You were a boy when I heard them, that's a fact—which doesn't prevent my being an old man now," rejoined Cesare Dias, with that shadow of melancholy in his voice which seemed so inconsistent with his character.

"What do years matter?" asked Anna, suddenly. "Other things matter much more; other things affect us more profoundly, more intimately, than years. Years are mere external, insignificant facts."

"Thanks for that kindly defence, my dear," Cesare Dias exclaimed, laughing; "but it only springs from the goodness of your heart."

"From the radiance of youth," said Luigi Caracciolo, bowing, to underline his compliment.

Anna was silent and agitated. Nothing so easily upset her equilibrium as light wordly conversation, based upon personalities and frivolous gallantry.

"Not enough, not enough," said Cesare Dias, wishing to cap the compliment, and at the same time to bring his own philosophy into relief. "As often as I find myself in the presence of these two girls, Luigi, who are two flowers of youthfulness, I seem to feel older than ever. I feel that I must be a hundred at least. How many changes of Government have I seen? Eight or nine, perhaps. Yes, I'm certainly more than a hundred, dear Anna."

And he turned towards her with a light ironical smile.

"Why do you say such things—such sad things?" murmured Anna.

"Indeed they are sad—indeed they are. Youth is the only treasure whose loss one may weep for the whole of one's life."

"But don't feel badly about it, dear Cesare. Consider. Isn't knowledge better than ignorance? Isn't the calm of autumn better than the storms of spring? You are our master—the master of us all. We all revere him, don't we, *Signorina*?" said Luigi, turning to Anna.

A shadow crossed Anna's face, and she let the conversation drop.

"And you, who say nothing, reasonable and placid Laura?" asked Cesare Dias. "Which is better—youth or age? Which is better—knowledge or ignorance? Here are knotty problems submitted to your wisdom, dear Minerva. You are a young girl, but you are also Minerva. Illuminate us. Who should be the happier—I, the master, or Caracciolo, my pupil?"

Laura thought for a moment, with an intent expression in her beautiful eyes, and then answered:

"It is best to combine the two—to have youth and wisdom together."

"The problem is solved!" cried Cesare Dias.

"And the *entr'acte* is over; everything in its time. Good evening, good evening; good-bye, Cesare," said Luigi.

So Caracciolo took his leave, very correctly, without shaking hands with Dias. Dias had risen, but Luigi seemed to understand that he meant to stay in the girls' box.

Anna, who had been looking up anxiously, waiting, looked down again now, reassured. The door closed noiselessly upon the young man.

"A pleasant fellow," observed Cesare Dias.

"Very pleasant," agreed Stella Martini, for politeness' sake, or perhaps because she desired to state her opinion.

"In my quality of centenarian I feel at liberty to stop where I am," said Cesare Dias, reseating himself behind Anna, while beside him, behind Laura, sat Stella Martini.

"You won't get a good view of the stage from there," said Stella.

"I don't care to see. It will be enough to hear it, this fourth act."

Anna said nothing. Courtesy forbade her looking directly at the scene, for thus she must have turned her back upon Cesare Dias. It embarrassed her a little to feel him there behind her. She did not move. Their two chairs were close together; and their two costumes made a striking contrast: his black dress-suit, the modern and elegant uniform of the man of the world, so austere and so handsome in its soberness; and her gown of white silk, the ceremonial robe of a young girl in society.

She was afraid her arm might touch Cesare's. He held his opera-hat in his hand. She forbore to fan herself, lest he might have to change his position. Now and then she raised her handkerchief to her lips, as if to refresh them with the cool linen.

While Saint-Bris, stirred by fanaticism, was telling the Catholic lords of the excesses of the Huguenots, and exciting them by his eloquence to share his fury; while the noble Nevers, the husband of Valentina, was protesting against the massacre; while, through the silence of the theatre, the grand musical poem of hatred, of wrath, of generosity, of love, and of piety, was surging up to the fascinated audience, Anna was thrilling at the thought that Cesare Dias was looking at her, at her hair, at her lips, at her person; she felt that she was badly dressed, pale, awkward, stupid. Wasn't the Contessa d'Alemagna a thousand times more beautiful than she? The Contessa d'Alemagna, with her dark complexion and her blue eyes, and her expression of girlish ingenuousness deliciously contrasted with womanly charm; the Contessa d'Alemagna, whom Cesare Dias had visited before coming to his ward's box. Weren't there a hundred women of their set present in the theatre this evening, each of them lovelier than she? Young girls, smiling brides, and ladies to whom maturity lent a richer attraction, all of them acquaintances of Cesare Dias, who, from time to time, looked at them through his opera-glass. And, indeed, her own sister, the wise Minerva, was she not more beautiful, more maidenly, more poetical than Anna? Was it not because of her beauty, her pure profile, her calm smile, that Cesare had called her by that gracious name, Minerva?

Anna bowed her head, as if oppressed by the heat and by the music, but really from a sense of self-contempt and humiliation. There was a looking-glass behind her. She was sorry now that she hadn't made an inspection of herself in it, on entering the box. She had forgotten her own face. Fantastically, she imagined it as brown and scarred, and hideously pallid. Her white frock made it worse. She registered a silent vow that she would always hereafter wear black. Only blonde women could afford to dress in white.

"You have dropped your fan," said Cesare Dias, stooping to recover it.

He smiled as he handed it to her.

"Thank you," said she, taking the fan.

Presently she put it down on an empty chair next to her. Cesare Dias picked it up, and began to fan himself. Then he pressed it to his face.

"What is it perfumed with?" he asked.

"Heliotrope."

"I like it," he said, and put the fan down.

She was burning with a desire to take it, to touch what he had touched, but she dared not.

Cesare Dias leaned forward a little, to look at the stage. He was so close to her, it seemed to Anna that she could hear him breathe.

For her own part, a sort of intoxication, due no doubt in some measure to the passionate art of the great composer, whose music surged like a flood about her, had mounted from her heart to her brain; she was conscious of nothing save a great world of love, save the near presence of Cesare Dias. Her soul held a new and precious treasure, a new joy. She delighted herself with the illusion that the beating of her own heart was the beating of Cesare's. She forgot everything—the place, the time, the future, youth, age, beauty, everything; motionless, with her eyes cast down, she seemed to float in a wave of soft warm light, aware of one single sweet sensation, his nearness to her. She had forgotten the stage, the people round her, Stella Martini, her sister Laura; the music itself was only a distant echo; her whole being was concentrated in an ecstasy, which she hoped might never end. She did not dare to move or speak, lest she might thereby wake from her heavenly dream. She had again entered anew into the land of passion. She was one of those natures which, having ceased to love, begin again to love.

"I could die like this," she thought.

She felt that she could die thus, in a divine moment, when new love, young and strong, has not yet learned the lessons of sorrow, of shame, of worldly wickedness, that await it; it would be sweet to die with one's illusions undisturbed, to die in the fulness of youth, before one's ideals have begun to decay; to die loving, rather than to live to see love die.

So, on the stage, Raoul and Valentina, victims of an irrepressible but impossible passion, were calling upon Heaven for death, praying to be allowed to die in their divine moment of love. Anna, recoiling from the thought of the future, with its inevitable vicissitudes, struggles, tears, and disappointments, realised the fascination of death. Involuntarily, she looked at Cesare. He smiled upon her, and thereat she too smiled, like his faithful image in a mirror. And her sublime longing to die, disappeared before the reality of his smile.

She looked at him again, but this time he was intent upon the scene. Anna felt that her love was being sung for her by the artists there, by Raoul and Valentina.

Cesare said to her, "How beautiful it is!"

"It is beautiful," she murmured, bowing her head.

It seemed to her that his voice had been unusually soft. What was the reason? What commotion was taking place in his heart? She asked herself these questions, but could not answer them. She loved him. That was enough. She loved him; she could not hope to be loved by him.

The music ceased. The curtain fell.

"Have you ordered the carriage?" Cesare Dias asked of Stella Martini.

"Yes, for twelve o clock.

"If you'll wait for me a moment I'll go and get my overcoat."

The ladies were putting on their cloaks, when Cesare came back, wearing his hat and overcoat. He helped Stella on with hers, then Laura, then Anna.

And looking at the sisters, he said, "You ought to have your portraits painted, dressed like this. I assure you, you're looking extremely handsome. I speak as a centenarian."

Laura smiled; Anna looked down, embarrassed. Her trouble was increased when she saw Cesare politely offer his arm to Stella Martini. Had she hoped that he would offer it to *her*? He motioned to the girls to take the lead in leaving the box. Anna put her arm through Laura's and went out slowly.

He conducted them to their carriage, and when they were safely in it, "I shall walk," he said, "It's such a fine evening. Good-night."

In the darkness, as they drove home, Laura asked, "Did you see Giustino Morelli?"

"No, he wasn't there."

"What do you mean? He *was* there."

"For me, he wasn't there. Giustino Morelli is dead."

V.

Cesare Dias encouraged the attentions which his young friend Luigi Caracciolo was paying to his ward Anna Acquaviva. He encouraged them quietly, with the temperance which he showed in all things, not with the undisguised eagerness of a father anxious to marry off his daughter.

And yet he was certainly anxious to marry her off. He was anxious to hand his responsibilities over to a husband, to confide to the care of another the safeguarding of that ardent and fragile soul, which threatened at any moment to fall into emotional errors. A thousand symptoms that could not escape his observant eye, kept him in a state of secret nervousness about her. It was true, nevertheless, that she had greatly changed for the better. Thanks to his constant watchfulness, to his habit of reproving her whenever she betrayed the impulsive side of her nature, to his sarcasm, to his biting speech, she had indeed greatly changed in manner.

A desire to obey him, to please him, a painless resignation, a loving humility, showed themselves in everything she said and did.

He saw that she was making mighty efforts to dominate the impetuousness of her character; he saw that she listened with close attention to his talk, trying to reconcile herself to those perverse theories of his which pained her mortally. That was what he called giving her a heart of bronze, strengthening her against the snares and delusions of the world. If he could but deprive her of all capacity for enthusiasm he would thereby deprive her of all capacity for suffering, as well.

Cesare Dias congratulated himself upon this labour of his, glorifying himself as a sort of creator, who had known how to make over the most refractory of all metals, human nature. And yet his mind was not quite at ease.

Her docility, her obedience, her self-control, roused his suspicions. He began to ask himself whether the girl might not be a monster of hypocrisy, whether under her tranquil surface she might not still be on fire within.

But had she not always been a model of sincerity? Her very faults, had they not sprung from the truthfulness and generosity of her nature?

No; the hypothesis of hypocrisy was untenable. Cesare Dias was far too intelligent to believe that the intimate essence of a soul can undergo alteration. It was impossible that a soul so essentially truthful as Anna's should suddenly become hypocritical.

And yet he was not easy in his mind.

What profound reason, what occult motive, could be at the bottom of Anna's change of front? What was it that enabled her and persuaded her to withhold her tears, suppress her sobs, and master the ardour of her temperament?

Ah, no! Cesare Dias was not easy in his mind. He knew the strength of his own will, he understood his own power to rule people and to impose his wishes upon them; but that was not enough to account for the conditions that puzzled him. There must be something else.

He was not anxious about Laura. The wise and beautiful Minerva he could marry whenever he liked, to whomsoever he liked. He was sure that Laura would be able to take care of herself. He held the opinion, common to men of forty, that marriage was the only destiny proper for a young girl. And it was only by means of a marriage that he would be able to relieve himself of his weight of responsibility in respect of Anna Acquaviva.

So, as often as he decently could, he brought meetings to pass between Luigi Caracciolo and his wards: sometimes at the theatre, sometimes in the Villa Nazionale, sometimes at parties and dances; indeed, it would seldom happen that Cesare would speak to the girls in public, without the handsome young Luigi Caracciolo appearing a few minutes later.

There was probably a tacit understanding between the two men.

Anna seemed to be unconscious of what was going on. Whenever her guardian approached her, presenting himself with that elegant manner which was one of his charms, she welcomed him with a luminous smile, giving him her hand, gazing at him with brilliant, joyful eyes, listening eagerly to what he had to say, and by every action showing him her good-will. And when, in turn, Luigi Caracciolo followed, she gave him a formal handshake, and exchanged a few words with him, distantly, coldly. He would try his hardest to shine before her, to bring the talk round to subjects with which he was familiar; but their interviews were always so short! At the theatre, between the acts; at the Villa, walking together for ten minutes at the utmost; at a ball, during a quadrille; and always in the presence of Laura, or Stella, or the Marchesa Scibilla, the girls' distant cousin, who often chaperoned them; and always watched from afar by their guardian Cesare Dias.

The relations between Luigi Caracciolo and Anna Acquaviva were such as, save in rare exceptional cases, always exist between people of the aristocracy. They were founded upon conventionality tempered by a certain amount of sympathy. The rigorous code of our nobility forbids anything approaching intimacy. Luigi Caracciolo's courtship of Anna was precisely like that of every other young man of his world. During the Carnival, it became a little more pressing, perhaps; he began to take on the appearance of a man in love. It seemed as if he invented pretexts for seeing her every day.

Willingly or unwillingly, Cesare Dias was his accomplice. Luigi was becoming more and more attentive. If Anna mentioned a book, he would send it to her, with a note; he would underline the sentimental passages, and when he met her again would ask her opinion upon it. If she mentioned a friend of her childhood, he would interest himself in all the particulars of the friendship. He was burning to know something about her first love affair; he had heard it vaguely rumoured that she had had one, that it had ended unhappily, and been followed by a violent illness.

And, indeed, from the way in which she would sometimes suddenly turn pale, from certain intonations of her voice, from her habit of going off into day-dreams when something said or done seemed to suggest old memories to her, it was easy for him to see that she must have passed through some immense emotional experience, and suffered from some terrible shock. She had a secret! Behind her great black eyes, behind her trembling lips, behind her silence, she hid a secret.

Luigi was in love with her, in his own way; not very deeply in love, but in love.

If Cesare Dias, in Anna's hearing, spoke of love, of the folly of passion, of the futility of hope, the girl bowed her head, listening without replying, as if she considered Cesare the infallible judge of all things.

Luigi Caracciolo saw this, and it tormented him with curiosity. Once he openly asked Dias if Anna had not already been in love. Dias, with the air of a man of the world, answered:

"Yes, she was interested in a young man, a decent young fellow, who behaved very well."

"Why didn't they marry?"

"The young man was poor."

"Was she very fond of him?"

"A mere girlish fancy."

"And now she has quite forgotten him?"

"Absolutely, absolutely."

This dialogue relieved Luigi for a moment; but he soon felt that it could not have contained the whole truth. He felt that the whole truth could only be told by Anna Acquaviva herself. And when he was alone with her he longed to question her on the subject, but his questions died unspoken on his lips.

Luigi's attentions to her had by this time become so apparent, and Cesare's manner was so much that of a father desirous of giving his consent to the betrothal of his daughter, that Anna could no longer pretend not to understand. Sometimes, when Cesare would come up to her, arm in arm with his young friend, she would look into his eyes with an expression which seemed to ask, "Oh, why are you doing this?"

He would appear not to notice this silent appeal. He knew very well that to attain his object he would have to overcome tremendous obstacles; that to persuade Anna Acquaviva to marry Luigi Caracciolo would be like taking a strong fortress. But he was a determined man, and he had determined to succeed. He saw her humility, he saw how she lowered her eyes before him, he felt that in most things she would be wax under his hand. But he was not at all sure that she would obey him when it came to a question of love, when it came to a question of her marriage. She might again rebel, as she had already rebelled.

Anna felt a latent irritation at perceiving Luigi's intentions and Cesare's approval of them, and she revenged herself by adopting towards the young man a demeanour of haughty politeness, against which he was defenceless. She took pleasure in contradicting him. If he seemed sentimental—and he was often sentimental in his way, which involved an element of sensuality—she became ironical, uttering paradoxes against sentiment in general; her voice grew hard; she seemed almost cynical. From sheer amiability Luigi Caracciolo always ended by agreeing with her, but it was easy to see that in doing so he was obeying his affection for her; he had quite the air of saying that she was right, not because he was convinced, but because she was a charming woman of whom he was devotedly fond.

"You agree with me for politeness' sake. What weakness!" she said angrily, with the impatience that women take no pains to conceal from men whom they don't like.

The slight smile with which Luigi assented to this proposition, and implied, moreover, that weakness born of a desire to please a loved one, was not altogether reprehensible, annoyed her more than ever. Anna wished the whole exterior world to keep tune to her own ruling thought, and anybody who by any means prevented such a harmony became odious to her. Such an one was Luigi Caracciolo.

Cesare Dias, with his acute insight, watched the couple rather closely. And when he saw Anna trying to avoid a conversation with Luigi, refusing to dance with him, or receiving him with scant courtesy, a slight elevation of his eyebrows testified to his discontent.

One day, when she had turned her back upon the young man at a concert, Cesare Dias, coming up, said to her, "You appear to be treating Caracciolo rather badly, Anna."

"I don't think so," she replied, trembling at his harsh tone.

"I think so," he insisted. "And I beg you to be more civil to him."

"I will obey you," she answered.

For several days after that she seemed very melancholy. Laura, who continued to sleep in the same room with her, often heard her sighing at night in her bed. Two or three times she had asked a little anxiously, "What is the matter?"

"Nothing, nothing. Go to sleep," Anna replied.

On the next occasion of her meeting Caracciolo, she treated him with exaggerated gentleness, in which, however, the effort was very apparent. He took it as so much to the good. She persevered in this behaviour during their next few interviews, and then she asked Dias, triumphantly: "Am I doing as you wish?"

"In what respect?"

"In respect of Caracciolo."

"Do you need my approbation?" he asked, in surprise. "For politeness' sake alone you should be civil to the young man."

"But it was you who told me to be so," she stammered meekly.

"I merely told you what a young lady's duty is—that's all."

She bent her head contritely. She had made a great effort to please Cesare Dias, and this was all the recognition she got. However, she could not feel towards him the least particle of anger; and the result was that her dislike of Luigi Caracciolo took a giant's stride.

Luigi Caracciolo's name was in everybody's mouth; everybody talked about him to her—Laura, Stella Martini, the Marchesa Scibilla. She shrugged her shoulders, without answering. Her silence seemed like a consent; but it is easy to guess that it was really only a means of concealing her unpleasant thoughts.

When, however, it was her guardian who mentioned Caracciolo, vaunting not only his charm, but also the seriousness of his character, she became excessively nervous. She looked at him in surprise, wondering that he could speak thus of such a disagreeable and vulgar person, and smiling ironically.

One day, overcome by impatience, she asked: "But do you really take him so seriously?"

"Who?—Caracciolo?"

"Of course—Caracciolo."

"I take every man seriously, who deserves it; and he does, I assure you."

"I don't want to contradict you," she said, softly; "but that is not my opinion."

"Have you really an opinion on the subject?" he responded, with a slight inflexion of contempt.

"Yes, indeed, I have an opinion."

"And why?"

"Why, because——"

"The opinions of young girls don't count, my dear. You are very intelligent; there's no doubt of that. But you know absolutely nothing."

"But, after all," she exclaimed, "do you really wish to persuade me that Caracciolo is a clever man?"

"Certainly."

"That he has a heart?"

"Certainly," he answered, curtly.

"That he is sympathetic?"

"Certainly," he repeated for the third time.

"Well, well," she said, disconcerted. "I find him arid in mind, hard of heart, and often absurd in his manners. No one will ever convince me of the contrary. He's a doll, not a man. Such a creature a man! It doesn't require much knowledge to see through *him*!"

"It is quite unnecessary to discuss it, my dear," said Cesare Dias, icily. "We won't discuss it farther. I'm not anxious to convince you, and it doesn't matter. Think what you like of anybody. It's not my affair to correct your fancies. I have unlimited indulgence still at your disposal for your extravagances; but there's one thing I can't tolerate—ingratitude. Do you understand—I hate ingratitude?"

"But what do you mean?" she cried, in anguish.

"Nothing more. Good night."

He turned on his heel and went away. For ten days he did not reappear in the Acquaviva household. He had never before let so long an interval pass without calling, unless he was out of town. Stella Martini, not seeing him, ingenuously sent to ask how he was. He replied, through his servant, that his health was perfect and that he thanked her for her concern.

In reality, he was furious because in his first skirmish with Anna on the subject of Luigi Caracciolo she had beaten him; furious, not only because of the wounds his *amour-propre* had received, but because his schemes for the girl's marriage were delayed. His anger was mixed with certain very lively suspicions, lively, though as yet not altogether clear in substance. It was impossible that Anna's conduct should not be due to some secret motive. He began at last to wonder whether she was still in love with Giustino Morelli.

Meanwhile, he refrained from calling upon her, well aware that in dealing with women no method is more efficacious than to let them alone. And, indeed, Anna was already sorry for what she had said, not because it wasn't true, but because she felt that she had thereby offended Cesare Dias, perhaps very deeply. But what could she do, what could she do? That Cesare Dias should plead with her for another man! It was too much. She felt that she must no longer trust to time; she must take decisive action at once.

Cesare's absence caused her great bitterness. Her regret for what she had said was exceedingly sharp during the first few days. She realised that she had been wrong, at least in manner. She ought to have held her tongue when she saw his face darken, and heard his voice tremble with scorn. Instead, in her foolish pride, she had held up her head, and spoken, and offended him. For two days, and during the long watches of two nights, stifling her sobs so that Laura should not hear them, she had longed to write him a little note to ask his pardon; but then she had feared that that might increase his irritation. Mentally, she was constantly on her knees before him, begging to be forgiven, as a child begs, weeping. She believed, she hoped he would come back; on his entrance she would press his hand and whisper a submissive word of excuse. She had not yet understood what a serious thing his silent vengeance could be.

He did not call. And now a dumb grief began to take the place of Anna's contrition, a dumb, aching grief that nothing could assuage, because everything reminded her of its cause, his absence. Whenever she heard a door opened, or the sound of a carriage stopping in the street before the house, she trembled. She had no peace. She accused him of injustice. Why was he so unjust towards her, towards *her* who ever since that fatal day at

Pompeii had only lived to obey him? Why did he punish her like this, when her only fault had been that she saw the insignificance, the nullity, of Luigi Caracciolo? Every hour that passed intensified her pain. In her reserve she never spoke of him. Stella Martini said now and again, "Signor Dias hasn't called for a long time. He must be busy."

"No doubt," replied Laura, absently.

"No doubt," assented Anna, in a weak voice.

She was burning up with anxiety, with heartache, with suspicion, and with jealousy. Yes, with jealousy. It had never occurred to her that Cesare might have some secret love in his life, as other men have their secret loves, and as he would be especially likely to have his, for he was rich and idle. In her ingenuousness and ignorance, it had never occurred to her. It was as if other women didn't exist, or as if, existing, they were quite unworthy of his interest. But now it did occur to her. In the darkness of his absence the thought came to her, and took possession of her; and sometimes it seemed so infinitely likely, that she could scarcely endure it.

It was more than probable that amongst all the beautiful women of his acquaintance there was one whom he loved. It was with her that he passed his hours—his entire days, perhaps. That was why Anna never saw him! At the end of a week her distress had become so turbulent, that her head reeled, as it used to reel when she thought of flying with Giustino Morelli. As it used to reel then? Nay, more, worse than then.

In those days she had not felt the consuming fires of jealousy, fires that destroy for ever the purest joys of love. In those days the man she cared for was so absolute in his devotion to her, she had not tasted the bitterness of jealousy, a bitterness beyond the bitterness of gall and wormwood, a poison from whose effects those who truly love never recover.

But who was she, the woman that so powerfully attracted Cesare as to make him forget his child! The Contessa d'Alemagna, perhaps. Yes, it must be she—that dark lady, with the blue eyes, the wonderful toilets, the youthful colour, the vivacious manner; she was indeed an irresistible enchantress. Poor Anna! During Cesare's absence she learned all the phases of hope and fear, of torturing jealousy, of wretched loneliness. He did not come he did not come; perhaps he would never come again. What had he said? That he detested ingratitude, that he despised people who were ungrateful. Ungrateful—she! But how could he expect her to thank him for wishing to marry her to Luigi Caracciolo? Was she really ungrateful?

Three or four times she had written to him, begging him to come; now a simple little note; now a long passionate letter, full of contradictions, wherein, to be sure, the word "love" never appeared, but where it could be read between the lines; now a frank, short love-letter: but each in turn had struck her as worse than the others, as more trivial, more ineffectual; and she had ended by tearing them to pieces.

It was she who had put it into Stella Martini's head to send to inquire how he was; his curt response to that inquiry struck a chill to her heart: he was in town, and he was well. Then she would go out for long walks with Stella, in the hope of meeting him.

One afternoon in February, at last, she did meet him, thus, in the street.

"How do you do?" she said, nervously.

"Very well," he answered, with a smile.

"It's a long while since we have seen you," said Stella Martini.

"I hadn't noticed it."

"You haven't called for many days," said Anna, looking into his eyes.

"Many?"

"Eight days."

"Eight. Really? Are you sure?"

"I have counted them," she said, turning away her head, as if to look at the sea.

"I'm sure that's a great compliment." And he bowed gallantly.

"It wasn't a compliment. It was affection, it was gratitude."

"Good. I see you're in a better frame of mind. I'll call to-morrow."

When he had left them, Anna and Stella went on towards the Mergellina, walking more rapidly than before. Anna kept looking at the sea, with a slight smile upon her lips, a new colour in her cheeks. She buried her hands in her muff. Had he not pressed one of those hands at parting with her? Now and then she would look backwards, as if expecting to see him again; it was the hour of the promenade. She did see him again, indeed; but this time he was in a carriage, a smart trap of the Viennese pattern, driven dashingly by Luigi Caracciolo.

She saw them approaching from afar, swiftly. She bowed and smiled to both of them. Her smile was luminous with happiness; and Luigi Caracciolo imagined himself the cause of it, and drove more slowly; and Cesare Dias was pleased by it, for he took it as an earnest of her better frame of mind.

When Stella Martini asked her, "Shall we continue our walk or go home?" she answered, "Let us go home."

She had seen him; she had told him how anxiously she had counted the days of his absence; he had promised that he would call to-morrow. She had seen him again, and had smiled upon him. That was enough. She mustn't ask too much of Providence in a single day.

Anna went home as happy as if she had recovered a lost treasure. And yet Cesare Dias had been cold and distant. But what did that matter to Anna? She had got back her treasure; that was all. Again she would enjoy his dear presence, she would hear his voice, she would sit near to him, she would speak with him, answer him; he would come again every day, at his accustomed hour; she could please herself with the fancy that that hour was sacred to him, as it was to her. Nothing else mattered. It was true that she had met him by the merest chance; it was true, that had chance ordered otherwise, a fortnight might have passed without her seeing him. It was true, that he had taken no pains to bring about their meeting. It was true, also, that she and Stella had as much as begged him to call upon them. But in all this he had been so like himself, his conduct had been so characteristic, that Anna was glad of it. It was a great thing to have made her peace with him, without having had to write to him.

"Signor Dias was looking very well," said Stella Martini, "we shall see him to-morrow."

"Yes, to-morrow," said Anna, smiling.

"I missed him immensely during his long absence."

"So did I."

"You're very fond of him, aren't you?" Stella inquired ingenuously.

"Yes," answered Anna, after a little hesitation.

"He's so good—in spite of the things he says," observed the governess.

"He is as he is," murmured Anna, with a gesture.

When they got home, Laura noticed Anna's air of radiant joy. Anna moved about the room, without putting by her hat or muff.

At last she said, "You know, we met Dias."

"Ah?" responded Laura, without interest.

"He's very well."

"That's nothing extraordinary."

"He's coming to-morrow."

"Good."

But when he arrived the next day, it was Laura who received him. Anna, at the sound of the bell, had taken refuge in her own room.

"Oh, wise Minerva!" cried Dias, pressing her little white hand. "You are well. You are natural. You know no weakness. You, I am sure, haven't been counting the days of my absence. I understand. I am wise, too. We are like the Seven Sages of Greece."

She responded with a smile. Cesare Dias looked at her admiringly. Then Anna came. She was embarrassed; and red and white alternated in her cheek. She spoke nervously, and kept her eyes inquiringly fixed upon Cesare's face. He, on the other hand, was calm and superior. He behaved as if he had never been away. He had the good sense not to mention Luigi Caracciolo; and Anna, who was waiting for that name as for an occasion to show her submissiveness, was disconcerted. Dias appeared to have forgotten the ingratitude with which he had reproached her. He had the countenance of a man too magnanimous to bear a grudge. And Anna was more than ever disconcerted by such unmerited generosity. For several days he did not speak of Caracciolo; then, noticing how Anna said yes to every remark he made, little by little he began to reintroduce the subject. Little by little Caracciolo regained his position, became a new, an important member of their group. He returned to the attack, encouraged by the smile he had received that day in the Mergellina. His manner was more devoted than ever. He treated the girl as a loved object before whom he could pass his life kneeling. She could not control a movement of dislike at first seeing him, because it was he who had occasioned her quarrel with Cesare Dias; but Luigi did not notice it; and she soon got herself in hand, determined to treat him as kindly as she possibly could. It was a sacrifice she was making to please Cesare Dias. She closed her eyes to shut out the vision of the peril towards which she was advancing. She compromised herself with Luigi Caracciolo day after day. She compromised herself as a girl does only with the man she means to marry; accepting flowers from him, answering his notes, listening to his compliments; and at night, when she was alone, she would tremble with anger and with self-contempt, counting the steps she had made during the afternoon towards the great danger! But the fear of seeing Cesare Dias again absent himself for eight days, the fear that he might again pass eight days at the feet of the Contessa d'Alemagna, or at those of some other beautiful woman—this fear rendered her so weak that she went on, not knowing where she might stop, feeling that she was approaching the most terrible crisis of her life.

Cesare Dias, somewhat easier in his mind about the girl appeared to be pleased in a fatherly way by her conduct; it seemed as if he was watching his chance to speak the decisive word. Anna, dreading that word, had got into an overwrought nervous condition, where her humour changed from minute to minute. Now she would cry, now she would laugh, now she would blush, now she would turn pale.

"What's the matter?" asked Dias.

"Nothing," she answered, passing her hand over her eyes.

But at his question she smiled radiantly, and he felt that he had worked a little miracle.

He was a clever man, and he knew that he must strike while the iron was hot. He must attack Anna in one of her moments of meekness, or not at all. Luigi Caracciolo became more and more pressing; he loved the girl, and he told her so in every look he gave her. And time was flying. Everybody who met Anna congratulated her upon her engagement; and when she replied: "No, I'm not engaged," people shook their heads, smiling sceptically.

One afternoon, angry with Caracciolo because of a letter he had written to her, and which he insisted upon her answering, she said to Dias, who was talking with Laura:

"I want to speak to you."

"Good. And I want to speak to you."

"Then—will you call to-morrow?"

"Yes. In the morning."

He returned to his conversation with Laura.

All night long she prayed for strength and courage.

And when, the next morning, she was alone with him, too frightened to speak, she simply handed him Caracciolo's letter. He took it, read it, and silently returned it.

"What do you think of it?" she asked.

"Ah!" he exclaimed, as if he did not wish to express an opinion.

"Does it strike you as a serious letter?"

"Yes, it's serious."

"I may easily be mistaken," she said. "That is why I want to ask your advice. You—you know so much."

"A little," he assented, smiling.

They spoke very quietly, seated side by side, without looking at each other.

"Doesn't he strike you as bold?" she asked.

"Who? Caracciolo? For having written that letter?"

"Yes."

"No. People in love are always writing letters. They don't always send them, but they always write them."

"Ah, is that so?"

"He loves you, therefore he writes to you."

"He loves me?" she inquired, trembling.

"Of course."

"Are you sure?"

"Certainly."

"Has he told you so?"

"He has told me so."

"And what did you answer?"

"I? Nothing. He asked me nothing. He merely announced a fact. It's from you that he expects an answer."

"From me?" she exclaimed.

"Every letter calls for an answer."

"I shan't answer this one."

"Why not?"

"Because I have nothing to say to him."

"Don't you love him?"

"No."

"Not even a little? Don't you like him?"

"No, I don't love him, I don't even like him."

"I can't believe it," he said, very gravely, as if he saw before him an insurmountable obstacle.

"You deceive yourself then," said she.

"I see that you receive him kindly, that you speak to him politely, that you listen to his compliments, apparently with pleasure. That's a great deal for a young girl to do." And he lifted his eyebrows.

"I have done it to please you—because he is a friend of yours," she cried.

"Thank you," he cried, curtly.

Then befell a silence. She played with an antique coin attached to her watch-chain, and kept her eyes cast down.

"So," he began presently, "so you won't marry Luigi Caracciolo?"

"No. Never."

"He's a splendid fellow, though. He has a noble name, a handsome fortune. And he loves you."

"I don't love him, and I won't marry him."

"Love isn't necessary in marriage," said Cesare coldly.

"Not for others, perhaps. For me it is necessary," she cried, pained in the bottom of her heart by this apothegm.

"You know nothing about life, my dear. A marriage for love and a marriage for convenience are equally likely to turn out happily or unhappily. And of what use is passion? Of none."

She bowed her head, not convinced, obstinate in her faith, but respecting the man who spoke to her.

"If you don't care for Luigi Caracciolo, you ought to try not to see him."

"I will avoid him."

"But he will seek you."

"I'll stay in the house."

"He'll write to you."

"I have already said I won't answer him."

"He will persevere; I know him. The prize at stake is important. He will persevere."

"You will tell him that the marriage is impossible."

"Ah, no, my dear. I shan't be the bearer of any such ungracious message."

"Aren't you—aren't you my guardian?"

"Yes, I am your guardian. But I heartily wish Francesco Acquaviva had not chosen me. Frankly, I would prefer to be nothing to you."

"Am I—so bad?" she pleaded, with tears in her eyes.

"I don't know whether you are good or bad. I don't waste my time trying to make such distinctions. I only know that he's a fine young fellow, handsome and rich, who loves you, and that you, without a single earthly reason, refuse him. I know that he is anxious to marry you, in spite of the fact that you don't care for him, in spite of—pass me the word—in spite of the extravagance of your character. Excuse me, dear Anna, but I want to ask you whether you think it will be easy to find another husband?"

"How can I tell?"

"I ask, do you think another will be likely to ask you for your hand?"

"Excuse me. I don't understand," she said, turning pale, because she did understand.

"My dear, have you forgotten the past?"

"What past?" she demanded, proudly.

"Nothing but a flight from home, my dear. A day passed at Pompeii with a young man. Nothing else."

"Oh, heavens!" she sobbed, burying her face in her hands.

"Don't cry out, Anna. This is a serious moment. You must control yourself. Remember that what you did respectable girls don't do. Luigi Caracciolo knows nothing about it, or nothing definite. But a man who did know about it, wouldn't marry you, my dear. It's hard; it's cruel; but it's my duty to tell it to you. Marry him; marry Luigi. That is the advice of a friend, of a true friend, Anna. Marry Luigi Caracciolo."

"I committed a great fault," she said, in a dull voice, "but haven't you forgiven me, you and Laura?"

"Yes, yes. But husbands—but young men about to marry, don't pardon such faults. With what jealous care I have kept that secret! I have guarded it as if I were your father. And now you let a chance like this slip away! Not realising that such a chance may never come again! But another man, an equal of Caracciolo, where is he to be found?"

"It is true that I committed a great fault," she said, returning always to the same idea; "but my honour was untouched."

"I am the only person who knows that."

"It is enough for me that you know it."

"Anna, Anna, you're a foolish child; that's what you are. You fall in love with a penniless nobody, you escape from your home, you risk your honour, and you are saved by a miracle. Afterwards, you are ill, you get well, you forget the young beggar; and then when a fine fellow like Caracciolo falls in love with you, you refuse him. You're mad, Anna. Marry Luigi Caracciolo. I beg you to marry him."

"You can't ask me that," she murmured.

"Love is a fancy. Marry Caracciolo."

"I can't."

"But why not? It's not a sufficient reason to say that you don't love him."

"Look for another reason, then," she said.

"I'll find it."

Cesare Dias had spoken these words in a threatening tone, unusual to him. He rarely lost his temper.

After a long pause he asked, smiling sarcastically, "You are in love with some one else, I suppose?"

Anna did not answer. She wrung her hands and hid her eyes.

"Why don't you answer? You've fallen in love again, have you not?"

"Again? What do you mean?" she exclaimed.

"I mean that to explain your refusal of Luigi Caracciolo, you must be in love with some other man. You little girls believe that passion is everlasting. You believe in faithfulness that lasts, if not beyond the grave, at least up to its brink. Are you still in love with Giustino Morelli?"

"Oh, don't insult me like that," she cried, in a convulsion of sobs.

"Calm yourself," said he, studying her with cold curiosity, while she wept.

"For pity's sake, don't think that of me," she besought him; "Say anything that I deserve, but not that, not that."

"Calm yourself," repeated Dias. "We will speak of this another day."

"Listen, listen," she cried. "Don't go away yet. Forgive me, first, for having interfered with one of your plans. But marry Luigi Caracciolo—I can't, indeed I can't. I never can. You smile at my word *never.* You are right, the human heart is such a fickle thing. Forgive me. But you will see that I am not wrong. You will never never have any more trouble with me. I will be so obedient, so meek. I will do everything you wish. Compared to you I am such a little, poor, worthless thing."

She was weeping. Giustino Morelli and Luigi Caracciolo had disappeared from the conversation; only Cesare Dias and Anna Acquaviva remained in it. He listened with growing curiosity. If in one sense he had lost a battle, in another his vanity had gained a victory. A smile passed over his face.

"Don't cry," he said.

"Oh, let me cry. I am so unhappy, so miserable. I have played away my life so foolishly. But I didn't know. I swear to you, I didn't understand. Now all is over. I am a lost woman——"

"Don't exaggerate."

"Oh, you yourself said it. You are right. A respectable girl, who holds dear her honour, who is jealous of her reputation, doesn't fly from her home, doesn't throw herself into the arms of a man. You are right—you only—you are always right—you who are so wise. But if you knew—if you knew what it is like, this madness that springs up from my heart to my brain—if you knew how I lose my head, when my feelings get the better of me—you would be sorry for me."

"Don't cry any more," he said, very low.

"Ah, if tears could only wash out the past," she sighed.

"Good-bye, Anna," he said, rising.

"Don't go away." And she took his hand. "I haven't said anything to you yet. I haven't explained. You are going away angry with me. But you are right. The sooner it is finished the better. To-day I have no strength. I irritate you. Women who make scenes are always tiresome. But you ought to know, you ought. I will write to you—I will write everything. You permit me to, don't you? Say that you permit me. I can't live unless you let me write and tell you everything."

"Write," he said, softly.

"And you forgive me?"

"I have nothing to forgive. Write. Good-bye, Anna."

She sat down. Dias went away. Laura and Stella came into the room.

"Well, is the marriage arranged?" asked Stella, not noticing Anna's red eyes and pale cheeks.

"No. It will never be arranged."

An hour later Laura asked: "Are you in love with Cesare Dias?"

"Yes," answered Anna, simply.

VI.

Anna's letter to Cesare Dias ran thus:

"I don't know what name to call you by, whether by your own name, so soft and proud, or whether by that of Friend, which says so much, and yet says nothing. I don't know whether I should write here the word that my respect for you imposes upon me, or the word that my heart inspires. Perhaps I had better call you by no name at all; perhaps I ought not to struggle against the unconquerable superior will that dominates me. I am so poor a creature, I am so devoid of moral strength, that the best part of my soul is unconscious of what it does, and when I attempt to act, I am defeated from the outset; is it not true? Ah, there is never an hour of noble and fruitful battle in my heart! Only an utter ignorance of things, of feelings, a complete surrender to the sweetness of love, and, thereby, the loss of all peace, all hope!

"How you must despise me. You are just and wise. You can't help despising a poor weak thing like me, a woman whose heart is always open, whose imagination is always ready to take fire, whose changeable mind is never fixed, whose veins, though cured of their great fever, are still burning, as if her rebellious blood could do nothing but burn, burn, burn. If you despise me—and your eyes, your voice, your manner, all tell me that you do—you are quite right. I never seem to be doing wrong, yet I am always doing it; and then, when I see it, it is too late to make good my error, to recover my own happiness, or to restore that of others. Ah, despise me, despise me; you are right to despise me. I bend to every wind that blows, like a broken reed. I am overturned and rent by the tempest, for I know neither how to defend myself nor how to die. Despise me; no one can despise me as you can, no one has so good a right to do it.

"When you are away from me, I can think of you with a certain amount of courage, trusting to your kindness, to your charity, to forgive me my lack of strength. When you are away from me, I feel myself more a woman, braver; I can dream of being something to you, not an equal, no, but a humble follower in the things of the soul. Dreams, dreams! When you are with me, all my faith in myself disappears; I recognise how feeble I am, how extravagant, how incoherent; no more, never more, can I hope for your indulgence.

"I think of my past—justly and cruelly you reproached me with it—and I find in it such a multitude of childish illusions, such an entirely false standard of life and love, such a monstrous abandonment of all right womanly traditions, that my shame rushes in a flame to my face. Have you not noticed it?

"Before that fatal day at Pompeii—the first day of my real existence—I had a treasury of feelings, of impressions, of ideas, my own personal ones, by which my life was regulated, or rather by which it was disturbed; they were swept away, they were destroyed, they disappeared from my soul on that day. To you, who showed me how great my fault was, to you, who trampled down all that I had cared for, I bow my head, I bow my spirit. You were right. You are right. You only are right. You are always right. I want to convince you that I see the truth clearly now. Let me walk behind you, let me follow you, as a servant follows her master. Ah, give me a little strength you who are strong, you who have never erred, you who have conquered yourself and the world. Give me strength, you who seem to me the model of calmness and justice—above all hazards, because you have known how to suffer in silence, above all human joy, because you understand its emptiness; and yet so kind, so indulgent, so quick to forgive, because you are a man and never forget to be a man.

"You despise me, that is certain; for all strong natures must despise weakness. But it is also certain that you pity me, because I am buffeted about by the storms of life, without a compass, without a star. I have already once been wrecked; in that wreck I left behind me years of health and hope, the best part of my youthful faith. And now I am in danger of being wrecked again, utterly and for ever, unless you save me.

"Say what you will to me; do what you will with me. Insult me, after having despised me. But don't leave me to my weakness, don't withdraw your support from me. It is my only help.

"What shall I call you? Friend?

"Friend, I shall be lost if you do not save me, if you refuse to allow my soul to follow yours, strengthened by your strength, if you cast me out from your spiritual presence, if you do not give me the support that my life finds in yours. Friend, friend, friend, don't cast me off. Say what you will, do what you will, but don't separate me from you. If you do, I shall die. I, a beggar, knock at your door."

The letter continued—

"You wounded me profoundly when you said that it was perhaps Giustino Morelli, the man for whose sake I refused to marry Luigi Caracciolo. I can't hear the bare name of Morelli, without shuddering with contempt. It isn't that I am angry with him, no, no. It is that he does not exist for me; he is the vain shadow of a dead man. On the evening of "The Huguenots,"—ah me! that music sings constantly in my soul, I shall never forget it—he was there, and I didn't see him, I wouldn't see him. I don't hate him. He was a poor, weak fool; honest perhaps, for you have said so; but small in heart and mind! And thus my contempt for him is really contempt for myself, who made an idol of him. How was I ever able to be so blind? When I think of it, I wring my hands in desperation, for it was before him that I burned the first pure incense of my heart. I shall never forgive myself."

Cesare Dias read this letter twice through. Then he left his house to go about his affairs and his pleasures. Returning home, he read it for a third time. Thereupon he wrote the following note, which he immediately sent off.

"Dear Anna,—All that you say is very well; but I don't know yet who the man is that you love.—Very cordially, Cesare Dias."

She read it, and answered with one line: "I love you.—Anna Acquaviva."

Cesare Dias waited a day before he replied: "Dear Anna,—Very well. And what then?—Cesare Dias."

In the exaltation of her passion she had taken a step whereby she risked her entire future happiness; and she knew it. She had taken the humiliating step of declaring her love. Would Dias hate her? She had expected an angry letter from him, a letter saying that he would never see her again; instead of which she had received a colourless little note, neither warm nor cold, treating her declaration as he might have treated any most ordinary incident of his day.

That was the unkindest cut of all. Cesare Dias was simply indifferent. For her, love was a tragedy; for him, it was an ordinary incident of his day.

What to do now? She could not think. What to do? What to do? Had he himself not asked, with light curiosity: "And what then?" He had asked it with the sort of curiosity one might show for the continuation of a novel one was reading.

All night long she sobbed upon her pillow.

"What is the matter?" asked Laura, waking up.

"Nothing. Go to sleep."

In the morning she wrote to him again:

"Why do you ask me *what then*? I don't know; I cannot answer. God has allowed me to love a second time. I know nothing of 'then.' I only know one thing—I love you. Perhaps you have known it too, this long while. My eyes, my voice, my words wherein my soul knelt before you, must have told you that I loved you. Have you not seen me bow my proud head daily in humility before you? I began to love you that evening when we came home together from Pompeii, when my fever was beginning. Afterwards, my whole nature was transformed by my love of you. I don't ask you to love me. Perhaps you are bound by other loves, past loves. Perhaps you have never loved, and wish never to love. Perhaps I don't please you, either spiritually or bodily. What is passing in your mind? Who knows? I only know that you are strong and wise, that you never turn aside, that you follow your noble path tranquilly, in the triumphant calm of your greatness. Have you loved? Will you love? Who knows? All I ask is that you will let me love you, without being separated from you. I ask that you will promise to wish me well, not as your ward, not as your sister, but as a poor girl who loves you with all her soul and life. I don't ask you to change your habits in any way; the least of your habits, the least of your desires, is sacred to me. Live as you have always lived, only remember that in a corner of Naples there is a heart that finds its only reason for existence in your existence, and continue from time to time to give it a minute of your presence. My love will be a silent companion to you.

"Are you not the same man who said to me, with a voice that trembled with pity, in that dark, empty room at the inn in Pompeii, while I felt that I was dying—are you not the same man who said, *My poor child, my poor child*?

"You pitied me. You do pity me. You will pity me. I know it, I know it. And that is the 'then' of my love.

"Don't write to me. I should be afraid to read what you might write.

"Ah, how I love you! How I love you!

"ANNA ACQUAVIVA."

Cesare Dias was very thoughtful after he had read this letter. His vanity, the vanity of a man of forty, was flattered by it. And Anna's love, for the present, at any rate, seemed to be entirely obedient and submissive. But would it remain so? Cesare Dias had had a good deal of experience. Anna's he knew to be a proud and self-willed character; would it always remain on its knees, like this? Some day she would not be content only to love, she would demand to be loved in return.

He did not answer the letter. He was an enemy to letter writing in general, to the writing of love letters in particular; and, anyhow, what could he say?

For two days he did not call upon her. On the third day, he arrived as usual, at two o'clock.

Anna, during these days, had lived in a state of miserable suspense and nervousness.

"What is the matter with her?" Stella Martini asked of Laura.

"I don't know."

But the governess tormented her with questions, and at last she answered impatiently: "I think she is in love."

"Again?"

"Yes, again."

"And with whom?"

"She has never told me to tell you," cried Laura, leaving the room.

"What is the matter with you?" Stella asked of Anna. "You are suffering. Why do you conceal your sorrow from me?"

"If I am suffering, it's my own fault," said Anna. "Only God can help me."

"Can't I help you? You are in deep grief."

"Deep grief."

"You have placed your hopes where they can't be realised? Again?"

"Again."

"Why, dear? Explain it to me."

"Because it is my destiny, perhaps."

"You are young, beautiful, and rich. You ought to be the mistress of your destiny. It is only poor solitary people who have to submit to destiny."

"I am poorer than the poorest beggar that asks for alms in the street."

"Don't talk like that," said Stella, gently, taking her hand. "Tell me about it."

"I can't tell you about it, I can't. It is stronger than I am," said Anna, and her anguish seemed to suffocate her.

"Tell me nothing, then, darling. I understand. I'm only a poor servant; but I love you so. And I want to tell you, Anna, that there are no sorrows that can't be outlived."

"If Heaven doesn't help me, my sorrow will kill me."

"The only irremediable sorrow in this world is the death of some one whom we love," said Stella, shaking her head. "You will see."

"I would rather die than live like this."

"But is the case quite desperate? Is there no ray of light?"

"Perhaps."

"Is it a man on whom your hope depends?"

"Yes."

"Do I know him?"

But Anna put her fingers on her lips, to silence Stella. The bell had rung. And, at the sound of it, Stella heard a great sigh escape from Anna's breast.

"What is it?" she asked.

"Nothing, nothing," said Anna, passing her pocket-handkerchief over her face. "Go to the drawing-room."

"Must I leave you alone?"

"I beg you to. I am so upset. I want a minute of peace."

"And you will come afterwards?"

"I'll come when I can—when I am calm again."

Stella went slowly away. In the drawing-room she found Dias, who was showing a copy of the illustrated *Figaro* to Laura. Dias bowed and asked, "And Anna?"

"She will come presently."

"Is she well?"

"Not ill."

"Then she is not well?"

"I don't think so. But you will see for yourself."

He and Laura returned to the engravings in the *Figaro*, which were very good. Stella left them.

Anna entered the room. Her heart was beating wildly. She did not speak. She sat down at the opposite side of the table on which the newspaper was spread out.

Dias said, referring to the pictures, "They're very clever."

"Very clever," agreed Laura.

Dias bowed to Anna, smiling, and asking, "How do you do?"

"Well," she answered.

"Signora Martini told me that she feared you were not very well."

"It's her affection for me, that imagines things. I am quite well." In his tone she could feel nothing more than pity for her. "I am only a little nervous."

"It's the weather, the sirocco," said Dias.

"Yes, the sirocco," repeated Anna.

"You'll be all right when the sun shines," said he.

"When the sun shines, perhaps," she repeated mechanically.

Laura rose, and left the room.

After a silence, Cesare Dias said, "It is true, then, that you love me?"

Anna looked at him. She could not speak. She made a gesture that said yes.

"I should like to know why," he remarked, playing with his watch-chain.

She looked her surprise, but did not speak.

"Yes, why," he went on. "You must have a reason. There must be a reason if a woman loves one man and not another. Tell me. Perhaps I have virtues whose existence I have never suspected."

Anna, confused and pale, looked at him in silence. He was laughing at her; and she besought him with her gaze to have pity upon her.

"Forgive me, Anna. But you know it is my bad habit not to take seriously things that appear very serious to others. My raillery hurts you. But some day you must really try to tell me why you care for me."

"Because you are you," she said softly.

"That's a very profound reason," he answered smiling. "But it would require many hours of meditation to be understood. And, of course, you will always love me?"

"Always."

"May I say something that will pain you?"

"Say it," she sighed.

"It seems to me, then, that you are slightly changeable. A year ago you thought you loved another, and would love him always. Confess that you have utterly forgotten him. And in another year—what will my place be?"

But he checked himself. She had become livid, and her eyes were full of tears.

"I have pained you too much. Nothing gives pain like the truth," he said. "But there, smile a little. Don't you think smiles are as interesting as tears? You're very lovely when you smile."

And obediently she smiled.

"Well, then, this eternal love," he went on, "what are we to do about it?"

"Nothing. I only love you."

"Does that suffice?"

"I must make it suffice."

"You are easily satisfied. Will you always be so modest in your hopes?"

"The future is in the hands of God," said she, not having the courage to lie.

"Ah! that is what I want to talk about—the future. You are hoping something from the future. Otherwise you would not be satisfied. The future, indeed! You are twenty. You have never thought of my age, have you?"

"It doesn't matter. For me you are young."

"And I will come to love you? That is your hope?"

"I have asked for nothing. Don't humiliate me."

He bowed, slightly disconcerted.

He put his hand in his pocket and drew out a little portfolio in red leather, which he opened, drawing forth two or three letters.

"I have brought your letters with me. Letters are so easily lost, and other people read them. So, having learned their contents, I return them to you."

She did not take them.

"What!" he cried, "aren't you glad to get them back? But there's nothing women wish so much as to get back the letters they have written."

"Tear them up—you," she murmured.

"It's not nice to tear up letters."

"Tear them, tear them."

"As you like," he said, tearing them up.

She closed her eyes while he was doing it. Then she said with a sad smile:

"So, it is certain, you don't care for me?"

"I mustn't contradict you," he answered gallantly.

He took her hand to bid her good-bye.

Slowly she went back to her bedroom.

There she found Stella Martini.

"Do you remember, Stella, that day I left you in the Church of Santa Chiara?"

"Yes; I remember."

"Well, now I tell you this—never forget it. On that day I signed my own death-sentence."

VII.

The Villa Caterina was embowered amongst the flowering orange-trees of Sorrento. On the side towards the town the villa had a beautiful Italian garden, where white statues gleamed amidst green leaves, and where all day long one could listen to the laughing waters of fountains. From the garden a door led directly into a big drawing-room. On the other side of the house a broad terrace looked over the sea.

This was the summer home of the Acquaviva family. It was bigger and handsomer than the house in Naples. There was greater freedom, greater luxury, greater cheerfulness here, than in the gloomy palace of the Piazza dei Gerolomini. The girls were very fond of Villa Caterina, and their father, Francesco Acquaviva, had been very fond of it. He had named it for his wife. It was here that the couple had passed all the summers of their married life; it was here that Caterina Acquaviva had died. The girls had a sweet, far-away memory of their mother; in her room at the Villa she was almost like a living presence to them.

When the spring came Anna began to speak of going to Sorrento. She felt that if she could get away from Naples she might experience a change of soul. The broad light and ceaseless murmur of the sea would calm her and strengthen her. When Laura or Stella asked her, "What is the matter?" she would answer, "I don't like being *here*."

She said nothing of her great sorrow. She shut it into her heart, and felt that it was killing her by inches. She passed long hours in silent meditation, her eyes fixed vaguely upon the air; when spoken to, she would start nervously, and look at her interlocutor as if she had suddenly been called back from a distant land of dreams.

Those who loved her saw her moral and physical trouble. She stayed in the house day after day; she gave up her walks; she went no more to the theatre. She had lost her interest in the things that used to please her. She was very gentle, very kind to everybody. To Cesare Dias she showed an unfailing tenderness. She was often silent before him. When he spoke to her, she would reply with a look, a look of such deep melancholy that even his hard heart was touched. She was very different to the impetuous creature of former times.

When the spring came, with its languorous warmth, her weakness increased. In spite of all her efforts to conquer her desire to do so, she would spend long hours writing to Cesare. It was her only way of showing the love that was consuming her. It was a great comfort, and, at the same time, a great pain. She wrote at great length, confusedly, with the disorder and the monotony of a spirit in distress; and as she wrote she would repeat her written phrases aloud, as if he were present, and could respond. She wrote thrilling with passion, and her cheeks burned. But, after she had committed her letters to the post, she would wish them back, they seemed so cold, so absurd, so grotesque, and she cursed the moment in which she had put pen to paper.

Cesare Dias never answered her. How could she expect him to, indeed? Had he not torn her first letters up, under her eyes?

Whenever his servant brought him one of Anna's letters he received it with a movement of impatience. He was not altogether displeased, however. He read them with a calm judicial mind, amused at their "rhetoric," and forbore to answer them. He went less frequently to her house than formerly. They were rarely alone together now. But sometimes it happened that they were; and then, observing her pale face, her eyes red from weeping, he asked: "What is it? Why do you go on like this?"

"What do you wish me to do?" she returned.

"I want you to be merry, to laugh."

"That—that is impossible," she said, drooping her eyes to hide the tears in them.

And Dias, fearing a scene, was silent.

He was a man of much self-control, but he confessed to himself that he would not be able, as she was, to bear an unrequited love with patience.

Anna was a woman, a woman in the full sense of the word. She had hoped to win his heart; but now she relinquished hope. And one day, in May, she wrote him a letter of farewell; she would never write again; it was useless, useless. She bade him farewell; she said she would like to go away, go away from Naples to Sorrento, to the Villa Caterina, where her mother had loved and died.

She begged Laura and Stella to take her to Sorrento. And Stella wrote to Dias to ask his permission. He replied at once, saying he thought the change of air would be capital for Anna. They had best leave at once. He could not call to bid them good-bye, but he would soon come to see his dear girls at the Villa.

Stella said: "Dias has written to me."

"When?" asked Anna.

"Yesterday. He says he can't come to bid us good-bye, he's too busy."

"Of course—too busy. Will you give me the letter?"

"It's a very kind letter," said Stella. She saw that Anna's hand was trembling as it held the white paper. Anna did not return it.

"Dias is very kind," said Anna.

They left Naples on the last day of May.

When they reached the villa, the two girls went directly to their mother's room. Laura opened the two windows that looked out upon the sea and let in the sunlight, and she moved from corner to corner, taking note of the dust on the furniture. Anna knelt at the praying-desk, above which hung a cross, an image of the Virgin, and a miniature of her mother.

Laura asked:

"Are you going to stay here?"

Anna did not answer.

"When you come away bring me the key," said the wise Minerva, and went off, softly closing the door behind her.

"Where is Anna?" asked Stella.

"She is still up there," said Laura.

"What is she doing?"

"Weeping, or praying, or thinking. I don't know."

"Poor Anna," sighed Stella.

How long did Anna remain on her knees before the image of the Virgin and the portrait of her mother? No one disturbed her. She kept murmuring: "Oh, Holy Virgin! Oh, my mother!" alternately.

When she came away, having closed the windows and locked the door, she was so pale that Stella said:

"You have stayed up there too long. It has done you harm."

"No, no," Anna answered; "I am very well; I am so much better. I am glad we have come here. I should like to live here always."

But Stella was not reassured. And at night the thought of her pupil troubled her and would not let her sleep. Sometimes she would get up and go to the door of Anna's room. There was always a light burning within. Two or three times she had entered; Anna lay motionless on her bed, with her eyes closed. Then Stella had put out the light.

"Why do you leave your light burning at night?" she asked Anna one day.

"Because I am afraid of the dark."

Thereupon Stella had prepared a little lamp for her, with a shade of opalescent crystal that softened its light; and almost every night Stella would go to Anna's room to see whether she was asleep. Her pale face in the green rays of the lamp had the semblance of a wreck slumbering at the bottom of the sea. Sometimes, hearing Stella's footsteps, Anna opened her eyes and smiled upon her; then relapsed into her stupor. For it was not sleep; it was a sort of bodily and mental torpor that kept her motionless and speechless. Stella returned to her own room, in no wise reassured. And what most worried this good woman was the long visit which Anna made every day to the room of her dead mother.

The villa was delightful during these first weeks of the summer, with its fragrant garden, its big, airy, cheerful, luxurious apartments, its splendid view of the sea. In the cool and perfumed mornings, in the evenings that palpitated with starlight, every window and balcony had its special fascination. But Anna saw and felt nothing of all this; her mother's room alone attracted her. There she passed long hours kneeling beside the bed, or seated at a window, silent, gazing off at the sea, with a white expressionless face. Sometimes Stella came to the door and called:

"Anna—Anna!"

"Here I am," she answered, starting out of her reverie.

"Come away; it is late."

"I am coming."

But she did not move; it was necessary to call her again and again.

Her stations there exhausted her. She would return from them with dark circles under her eyes, her lips colourless, the line of her profile sharpened and accentuated.

Stella felt a great pity for her, a great longing to be of help to her. She tried to persuade her to cut short her vigils in her mother's room.

"You ought not to stay so long. It is bad for you."

"No, no," Anna answered. "If you knew the peace I find there."

"But a young girl like you ought to wish for the excitements of life, not the peace."

"There are no more flowers for Margaret," quoted Anna, going to the window and looking towards the sea.

During the whole month of June, a lovely month at Sorrento, where the mornings are warm and the evenings fresh, Anna fell away visibly in health and spirits. Laura and Stella did not interfere with her, but it saddened them to witness her decline. Stella's anxiety was almost motherly. When she saw Anna's pale, peaked face, when she noticed her transparent hands, a voice from within called to her that she must do something for the poor girl.

One day she said, "Signor Dias has promised to come here for a visit. But he's delaying a little. Perhaps he'll come for the bathing season."

"You will see. He'll not come at all," replied Anna, her eyes suddenly filling with tears.

"He's so kind, and he has promised. He will come."

"I don't believe it," Anna answered sadly.

Indeed, he neither came nor wrote. The first fortnight of July had passed; the bathing season had already begun. Sorrento was full of people. In the evening, till late into the night, from every window, from every balcony, and from the big brilliantly lighted drawing-rooms of the hotels, came the sounds of singing and dancing, the tinkling of mandolines, the laughter of women—a gay, passionate, summer music. The villas were protected from the sun by blue and white striped awnings, which fluttered in the afternoon breeze like the sails of ships. At night the moon bathed houses, country, and sea in a radiance dazzling as snow. Anna, in the midst of all this merriment, this health and beauty, felt only the more profoundly a great longing to end her life. It was seldom now that she so much as moved from one room to another. In the evening, when Stella and Laura would go out to call upon their friends, Anna would seat herself in an easy-chair on the terrace of the Villa, and fix her eyes upon the sky, where the Milky Way trembled in light. And on the sea beyond her, people were singing in boats, or sending up fireworks from yachts. Round about her sounded the thousand voices of the glorious summer night, voices of joy, voices of passion. Anna neither saw nor heard.

But in Stella's face she could not help noticing an expression of sympathy which seemed to say, "I have divined—I have guessed." And in the kiss which Stella gave her, before going out, on the evening of the 17th of July, Anna felt an even deeper affection than usual. Laura and Stella were going to a dance at the Villa Victoria.

"Be strong and you will be happy," Stella said, and her kiss seemed meant as a promise of good news.

But the poor child did not understand. She took Stella's words as one of those vague efforts at consolation which people make for those who are inconsolable, and shook her head, smiling sadly. Lovely in her white frock, Laura too came and kissed her. And then she heard the carriage drive away. Anna left the drawing-room and went out upon the terrace. There was a full moon; its light was so brilliant one might have read by it. There was something divinely beautiful in the view—from the horizon to the arch of the sky, from the hills behind her, covered with olives and oranges, to the sea before her. And she felt all the more intensely the sorrow of her broken life.

She lay back in her easy-chair, with her eyes closed.

"Good evening," said Cesare Dias.

She opened her eyes, but she could not speak. She could only look at him, and she did so with such an expression of desolate joy that he told himself: "This woman really loves me."

He appeared to be very thoughtful. He drew up a chair, and sat down next to her.

"Are you surprised to see me, Anna? Didn't I promise to come?"

"I thought—that you had forgotten. It is so easy to forget."

"I always keep my promise," he declared.

When had she heard him speak like this before, with this voice, this inflexion—when? Ah, she remembered: when she was ill, when they thought she was going to die. So it was pity for one threatened with death that had brought him to Sorrento; it was pity that banished its habitual irony from his voice.

"The air of Sorrento hasn't cured you," he said, bending a little to look at her.

"It hasn't cured me. It has cured me of nothing. I think I shall never be cured. There is no country in the world that can cure me."

"There is only one doctor who can do you any good—that doctor is yourself."

He opened his silver cigarette-case, took out a cigarette, and lit it.

She watched the vacillating flame of his match, and for a moment did not speak.

"It is easy to say that," she went on finally, with a feeble voice. "But you know I am a weak creature. That is why you have so much compassion for me. I shall never be cured, Cesare."

"Are you sure?"

"I am sure. I have tried. My love has proved itself stronger than I. It is destroying me. My heart can no longer endure it."

He looked off into the clear air of the night, watching the spiral of his cigarette smoke.

"And all those beautiful spiritual promises," he said, "that wonderful structure of abnegation, of sacrifice, of unrequited love, has come to nothing! Those plans for the future, which you conceived in such lofty unselfishness, have failed?"

"Failed, failed," she exclaimed, with a sigh, gazing up at the starry sky, as if to reproach it with her own unhappiness. "All that I wrote to you was absurd, a passing illusion. All my plans were based upon absurdities. Perhaps there are people in the world who are so perfectly made that they can be contented to love and not be loved in return; they are fortunate, they are noble; they live only for others; they are purity incarnate. But I am a miserable, selfish woman, nothing else; I have expected too much; and I am dying of my selfishness, of my pride."

She raised herself in her chair, grasping its arms nervously with her hands, and shaking her beautiful head, wasted by grief.

He was silent. He threw away his cigarette, which had gone out.

The soft moonlight covered all things.

"I am so earthly," she went on. "I have prayed for a better nature, for an angelic heart, raised above all human desires, that I might simply love you, and wish for nothing else. I have exhausted myself with prayers and tears, trying thus to forget that you could not care for me. I have forbidden myself the great comfort of writing to you. I left Naples, and came here, far from you—from you who were, who are my light, my life. In vain, I have passed whole days here, praying to my mother and to the Madonna to free me from these terrible, heavy, earthly chains that bind me to that longing to be loved, and that are killing me. No use, no use! My prayers have not been answered. I have come away from them with a greater ardour, a more intense longing, than ever. I am a woman. I am a woman who doesn't know how to lift herself above womanly things, who, womanlike, longs to be loved, and who will never, never be consoled for the love she cannot have."

After a long pause, he asked, "And what do you wish me to do, Anna?"

"Nothing."

"Nothing?"

"There is nothing to be done. All is ended; all is over. Or, rather, nothing has ever been begun."

"Anna, I assure you, it grieves me to see you suffer."

"Thank you. But what can you do for me? It is all due to my own folly. I admit that I am unbalanced, extravagant. I know it. I am paying dearly for my folly; ah, the expiation is hard. It is all due to my one mistake, my one fault. Everybody is very kind to me, more than kind. But I have sinned, and I must expiate my sin."

"But how is it all to end?" he cried.

"Do you know what the simplest solution would be?"

"What?"

"My death. Ah, to rest! to rest for ever, under the earth, in a dark grave!"

"Don't say that. People don't die of love."

"Yes that is true. There is indeed no recognised disease called *love*. Neither ancient nor modern doctors are acquainted with it; they have never discovered it in making their autopsies. But love is such a subtle deceiver! It is at the bottom of all mortal illnesses. It is at the bottom of those wasting declines from which people suffer for years, people who have loved too much, who have not been loved enough. It is in those maladies of the heart, where the heart bursts with emotion or dries up with despair. It is in those long anæmias which destroy the body fibre by fibre, sapping its energies. It is in that nervousness which makes people shiver with cold and burn with insupportable heat. Oh, no one dies suddenly of love. We die slowly, slowly, of troubles that have so many names, but are really all just this—that we can endure to love no longer, and that we are not loved. Who will ever know the right name of the illness from which I shall die? The doctor will write a scientific word on paper, to account for my death to you, to Laura, to Stella. But you know, you at least, that I shall die because you do not love me."

"Calm yourself, Anna."

"I am calm. I have no longer the shadow of a hope. But I am calm, believe me. I have to tell you these things because they well up from my soul of their own accord. I am an absolutely desperate woman, but I am calm, I shall always be calm. Don't answer me. Everything that you can say I have already said to myself. All is ended. Why should I not be calm?"

"But, if you no longer hope for anything, then you have hoped for something. For what?" he asked, with a certain curiosity.

"Oh, heavens!" she cried. "That you should ask me that!"

"Tell me, Anna. You see that I ask it with sympathy, with lively sympathy."

"But you must have forgotten what love is like, if you ask me to tell you what its hopes are," she exclaimed. "One hopes for everything when one loves. From the moment when I first trembled at the sound of your voice, from the moment when first the touch of your hand on mine thrilled me with delight, from the moment when first the words you spoke, whether they were hard or kind, scornful or friendly, seemed to engrave themselves upon my spirit, from the moment when I first realised that I was yours—yours for life, from that moment I have hoped that you might love me. From that moment it has been my dream that you might love me, with a love equal to my own, with a self-surrender equal to my own, with an absolute concentration of all your heart and soul, as I love you. That has been the sublime hope that my love has cherished."

"It was an illusion," he said softly, looking off upon the broad shining sea, bathed in the moonlight.

"I know it. Why do you remind me of it? Why are we talking of it? My soul had fallen into a torpor. But now you rouse me from it. My heart throbs as if you had reopened its wound. Don't tell me again that you don't care for me. I know it, I know it."

"Anna, Anna, why do you torment yourself like this?"

"Ah, yes, I have known it a long while now. My great hope died little by little, day by day, as I saw how unlike me you were, how far from me; as I understood your contempt for me, your pity; as I realised that there were secrets in your life which I could not know; as I perceived that the differences of our ages and tastes had bred differences of feeling. In a hundred ways, voluntarily and involuntarily, you showed me that love did not exist for you, either that you would never love, or, at any rate, that you would never love me. I read my sentence written in letters of flame on my horizon. And yet, you see, in spite of the blows that fate had overwhelmed me with, I was not resigned. I told myself that a young and ardent woman could not thus miserably lose herself and her love. I thought that there was a way of saving herself which ought to be tried, a humble way, but one that I could pursue in patience. Shall I tell you my other dream?"

"Yes, tell me."

"Well, I dreamed that you would let me unite my weak and stormy youth to your warm and serene maturity, in such a manner as to complete more profoundly and more intimately the work of protection that Francesco Acquaviva had confided to you at his death. You saved me at Pompeii. That seemed to sanction a supreme act of devotion on my part. My dream was simple and modest. I would love you with all my strength, but in silence; I would live with you, loving and following you like a fond shadow. Every hour, every minute, I would be able to offer you unspoken, but eloquent proofs of my love. I would be your satellite, circling round you, drinking in the light of my sun. I would watch my chance to do for you, to serve you, to make you happy. And in this way, never asking for gratitude, asking for nothing, I would spend my life, to its last day, blessing you, worshipping you, for your kindness in letting me be near you, in letting me love you. Ah, what a vision! It would be worthy of me, to make such a sacrifice of every personal desire; and worthy of you to lift a poor girl up to the happiness of seeing you every day, of sharing your home and your name."

"You would like me to marry you?" asked Dias.

"Your wife, your mistress, your friend, your servant—whatever you wish will suffice for me. To be where you are, to live my life out near to you——"

"I am old," he said, coldly, bitterly.

"I am young, but I am dying, Cesare."

"Old age is a sad thing, Anna. It freezes one's blood and one's heart."

"What does it matter? I don't ask you to love me. I only want to love you."

"Will you never ask it of me?"

"Never."

"Promise."

"I promise."

"By whatever you hold most sacred, will you promise it?"

"By Heaven that hears me, by the blessed souls of my mother and father who watch over me; by my affection for my sister Laura; by the holiest thing in my heart, that is, by my love for you, I promise it, I swear it, I will never ask you to love me."

"You won't complain of me, and of my coldness?"

"I will never complain. I will regard you as my greatest benefactor."

"You will let me live as I like?"

"You will be the master. You shall dispose of your life and of mine."

"You will let me go and come, come and go, without finding fault, without recriminations?"

"When you go out I will await in patience the happy hour of your return."

He was silent for a moment. There was another question on his mind, and he hesitated to ask it. But with burning eyes, with hands clasped imploringly, she waited for him to go on.

"You won't torment me with jealousy?" he asked at last.

"Oh, heavens!" she cried, stretching out her arms and beating her brow with her hands; "must I endure that also?"

"As you wish," he said, coldly. "I see that I displease and offend you. I am making demands that are beyond your strength. Well, let us drop the subject."

And he rose as if to go away. She moved towards him and took his hand.

"No, no; don't leave me. For pity's sake stay a little longer. Let us talk—listen to me. You ask me not to be jealous; I'll not be jealous. At least, you'll not see my jealousy. Do you wish me to visit the woman you're in love with, or have been in love with, or the woman who's in love with you? Do you wish me to receive the women who are your friends? I'll do it—I'll do everything. Put me to the most dreadful trial—I'll endure it. Ask me to go to the furthest pass a soul and body can reach—I'll do it for you."

"I wish to be free, heart-free, that is all," he said, firmly.

"As you are to-day, so you will always be—free in heart," she responded.

"Listen to me, Anna, and understand me clearly. For a moment try to escape from your own personality, forget that you are you, and that you love me. For a moment consider calmly and carefully the present and the future. Anna, I am old, and you are young; and the discrepancy of our ages which now seems trifling to you, in ten years' time will seem terrible, for I can only decline, while you will grow to maturity. In your imagination you have conceived an ideal of me which doesn't correspond to the truth, and which the future will certainly correct, to your sorrow. Between our characters and our temperaments there is a profound gulf; we have no reason to believe that the future can close it up. If I am making a sacrifice, as I confess I am, in speaking to you thus, it is certain that you would make a more painful and a more lasting one in living with me. Think of it, think of it. Think of my age, of your illusions which must inevitably be destroyed, of our mutual sacrifice. Anna, there is still time."

She looked at him, surprised to hear him speak in this earnest way, the man who was accustomed to dominate all his own emotions. He was really moved; his brow was knitted; and on it, for the first time, Anna could read a secret distress. There was something almost like shyness in his eyes; he seemed less distant, less strong perhaps, than he had ever seemed to her before, but more human, more like other people, who suffer and weep.

"Anna, Anna," he went on, "put aside all selfishness, and be yourself the judge. Judge whether I ought to consent to what you wish. I have told you cruelly, brutally, what I shall expect from you in return from my sacrifice. I have repeated to you again and again what a grave step it is that you propose. Now, my dear child be calm, and judge for yourself."

She was leaning with her two hands on the parapet of the terrace, and kept her eyes cast down.

"But why," she asked slowly, in a low voice, "why are you willing—you who are so wise, so cold, who despise all passion, as you do—why are you willing to make this sacrifice? Who has persuaded you? Who has won you?"

"I am willing because you have told me that there is no other way of saving you; because Stella Martini has written to me saying that I ought to save you; because I myself feel that I ought to save you."

"It is for pity then that you are willing to do this thing?"

"You have said it," he replied, not wishing to repeat the unkind word.

"God bless you for your pity," she said humbly, crossing her hands as in prayer.

There was a deep silence. He stood with his head bowed, thinking, and waiting for her to speak. She was looking at the sky as if she wished to read there the word of her destiny. But in her heart and in her mind, from the sky, and from the glorious landscape, only one word could she, would she, hear.

"Well, Anna, what have you to say?"

"Why do you ask? I love you, and without you I should die. Anything is better than death. You are my life."

"Then you will be my wife and my friend," he said resolutely.

"Thank you, love," and she knelt before him.

When he had gone away, she bent down and kissed devotedly the wall of the terrace, where he had leaned, speaking to her.

And then she went to each of the big vases that stood in a row along the terrace, and picked all the flowers that grew in them, the roses, the geraniums, the jasmine-buds, and pressed them to her bosom in a mass, because they had listened to her talk with him. And before re-entering the house, she looked again, with brilliant eyes full of happiness, upon the sea and the sky and the wide moonlit landscape.

Within the house every one was asleep. The servant who was sitting up for Laura and Stella nodded in the anti-chamber. Anna was quite alone, and her heart danced for joy.

Silently she passed through the house, and entered her mother's room.

"Oh, Mamma, Mamma, it is you who have done this," she said.

END OF PART I.

PART II

I.

Anna wore a pink dressing-gown of soft wool, with a low-cut sailor's collar and monk's-sleeves, so that her throat and wrists, round and pale with the warm pallor of ivory, were left uncovered. Her hair was drawn up in a rich mass on the top of her head, and confined by two or three pins of yellow tortoise-shell. Her black eyes were radiant with youth and love.

She opened the door of her room.

She had a little clock in a case of blue velvet lightly ornamented with silver; Cesare had given it to her during their honeymoon, and she always kept it by her. She looked at this, and saw that it was already eleven. The April sunshine poured merrily into the room, brightening the light colours of the upholsteries, touching with fire her bronze jewel-case, her hanging lamp of ancient Venetian wrought iron, and the silver frame of her looking-glass, and giving life to the blue forget-me-nots on the white ground of her carpet.

It was eleven. And from the other end of the apartment (where, with Stella Martini she occupied two or three rooms) Laura had sent to ask at what hour they were to start for the Campo di Marte. Anna had told the servant to answer that they would start soon after noon, and that she was getting ready.

For a moment she stood still in the middle of her room, undecided whether or not to move in the direction that her feet seemed inclined to take of their own will—pretty little feet, in black slippers embroidered with pearls.

Then she opened the door.

A short passage separated her room from her husband's. Her husband's room had a second door, letting into a small hall, whence he could leave the house without Anna's knowing it, without her hearing so much as a footstep.

She crossed the passage slowly, and leaned against the door, not to listen, but as if she lacked courage to knock. At last, very softly, she gave two quick raps with her knuckles.

There was a minute of silence.

She would never have dared to knock a second time, already penitent for having ventured to disturb her lord and master.

A cold quiet voice from within inquired, "Who is it?"

"It's I, Cesare," she said, bending down, as if to send the words through the keyhole.

"Wait a moment, please."

Patiently, with her bejewelled hand on the knob, and the train of her pink dressing-gown heaped about her feet, she waited. He never allowed her to come in at once, when she knocked at his door, he seemed to take a pleasure in prolonging and subduing her impatience.

Presently he opened the door. He was already dressed for the Campo di Marte, in the appropriate costume of a lover of horse-racing.

"Ah, my dear lady," he said, bowing with that fine gallantry which he always showed to women, "aren't you dressed yet?"

And as he spoke he looked at her with admiring eyes. She was so young and fresh, and living, with her beautiful round throat, her flower-like arms issuing from her wide monk's sleeves, and her tiny feet in their black slippers, that he took her hand, drew her to him, and kissed her on the lips. A single kiss; but her eyes lightened softly, and her red lips remained parted.

He stretched himself in an easy-chair, near his writing-desk, and puffed a cigarette. All the solid and simple yet elegant furniture of the big room which he occupied, was impregnated with that odour of tobacco, which solitary smokers create round themselves like an atmosphere.

Anna sat down, balancing herself on the arm of a chair covered with Spanish leather. One of her feet played with the train of her gown. She looked about, marvelling as she always did, at the vast room a little bleak with its olive plush, its arms, its bookcase, its handful of books in brown bindings, and here and there a bit of carved ivory or a bright-coloured neck-tie, and everywhere the smell of cigarette-smoke. His bed was long and narrow, with a head-piece of carved wood; its coverlet of old brocade fell to the floor in folds, and mixed itself with the antique Smyrna carpets that Cesare Dias had brought home from a journey in the East. Attached to the brown head-piece there was a big ivory crucifix, a specimen of Cinquecento sculpture, yellow with age. The whole room had a certain severe appearance, as if here the gallant man of the world gave himself to solitary and austere reflections, while his conscience took the upper hand and reminded him of the seriousness of life.

The big drawers of his writing desk surely contained many deep and strange secrets. Anna had often looked at them with burning, eager eyes, the eyes of one anxious to penetrate the essence of things; but she had never approached them, fearing their mysteries. Only, every day, after breakfast, when her husband was away, she had put a bunch of fresh, fragrant flowers in a vase of Satsuma, whose yellow surface was crossed by threads of gold, and placed them on the dark old desk, which thereby gained a quality of youth and poetry. He treated the flowers with characteristic indifference. Now and then he would wear one of them in his button-hole; oftener he seemed unconscious of their existence. For a week at a time jonquils would follow violets and roses would take the place of mignonette in the Satsuma vase, but Cesare would not deign to give them a look. This morning, though, he had a tea-rose bud in his button-hole, a slightly faded one that he had plucked from the accustomed nosegay; and Anna smiled at seeing it there.

"At what time are we going to the races?" she asked, remembering the business that had brought her to his room.

"In about an hour," he answered, looking up from a memorandum-book in which he was setting down certain figures with a pencil.

"You are coming with us, aren't you?"

"Yes. And yet—we shall look like a Noah's ark. Perhaps I'd better go with Giulio on the four-in-hand."

"No, no; come with us. When we are there you can go where you like."

"Naturally," he said, making another entry in his note-book.

She looked at him with shining eyes; but he continued his calculations, and paid her no attention. Only presently he asked:

"Aren't you going to dress?"

"Yes, yes," she answered softly.

And slowly she went away.

While her maid was helping her to put on her English costume of nut-coloured wool, she was wondering whether her husband would like it; she never dared to ask him what his tastes were in such matters; she tried to divine them. Before dressing, she secured round her throat by a chain an antique silver reliquary, which enclosed, however, instead of the relics of a saint, the only love letters that he had ever written to her, two little notes that had given her unspeakable pain when she had received them. And as she moved about her room at her toilet, she cast repeated glances at his portrait, which hung over her writing-table. Round her right arm she wore six little golden bracelets with pearls suspended from them; and graven upon each bracelet was one letter of his name, Cesare. Her right hand gleamed with many rings set with precious stones; but on her left hand her wedding-ring shone alone.

When she had adjusted her veil over her English felt hat, trimmed with swallows' wings, she looked at herself in the glass, and hesitated. She was afraid she wouldn't please him; her dress was too simple; it was an ordinary morning street costume.

Suddenly the door opened, and Laura appeared. As usual, she wore white, a frock of soft white wool, exquisitely delicate and graceful. Her hat was covered with white feathers, that waved with every breath of air. And in her hands she held a bunch of beautiful fresh tea-roses.

"Oh, how pretty you are!" cried Anna. "And who gave you those lovely roses?"

"Cesare."

"Give me one—give me one." And she put out her hand.

She put it into her button-hole, inexpressibly happy to possess a flower that he had brought to the house and presented to her sister.

"When did you see Cesare?" she asked, taking up her purse, across which *Anna Dias* was stamped, and her sunshade.

"I haven't seen him. He sent these flowers to my room."

"How kind he is."

"Very kind," repeated her sister, like an echo.

They went into the drawing-room and waited for Cesare. He came presently, drawing on his gloves. He was somewhat annoyed at having to go to the races with his family—he who had hitherto always gone as a bachelor, on a friend's four-in-hand, or alone in his own phæton. His bad humour was only partially concealed.

"Ah, here is the charming Minerva!" he cried, perceiving Laura. "How smart we are! A proper spring toilet, indeed. Good, good! Well, let's be off."

Anna had hoped for a word from him too, but she got none. Cesare had seen her dress of nut-coloured wool, and he deemed it unworthy of remark. For a moment all the beauty of the April day was extinguished, and she descended the stairs with heavy steps. But out of doors the air was full of light and gaiety; the streets were crowded with carriages and with pedestrians; on every balcony there were ladies in light colours, with red parasols; and a million scintillating atoms danced in every ray of sunshine. Anna told herself she must bear in patience the consequences of the error she had made in putting on that ugly brown frock. Laura's face was lovely as a rose under her white hat; and Anna rejoiced in her sister's beauty, and in the admiring glances that everybody gave her.

"It's going to be beastly hot," said Cesare, as they drove into the Toledo, where a crowd had gathered to watch the procession of carriages.

"The Grand Stand will be covered. We'll find a good place," said Anna.

"Oh, I'm to leave you when we get there," he reminded her. He was determined to put an end to this family scene as soon as he could. "I must leave a clear field for Laura's adorers. I give place to them because I am old."

Laura smiled.

"So, Anna, I'll leave you to your maternal duties. I recommend you to keep an especial eye upon Luigi Caracciolo—upon him in particular."

"What do you mean?" Anna asked absently.

"Nothing, dear."

"I thought——" she began, without finishing her sentence.

Bows and smiles and words of greeting were reaching them from every side. They passed or overtook numberless people whom they knew, some in carriages, some on foot. Cesare was inwardly mortified by the conjugal exhibition of himself that he was obliged to make, and looked with secret envy at his bachelor friends.

But his regret was sharpest when a handsome four-in-hand dashed past, with Giulio Carafa on the box and the Contessa d'Alemagna beside him. That dark, vivacious, blue-eyed lady wore a costume of pale yellow silk, and a broad straw hat trimmed with cream-coloured feathers. She carried a bunch of lilac in her hands, lilac that lives but a single day in our ardent climate, and is rich with intoxicating fragrance. All the men on Carafa's coach bowed to Dias, and the Contessa d'Alemagna smiled upon him and waved her flowers; and his heart was bitten by a great desire to be there, with them, instead of here, in this stupid domestic party.

He was silent; and Anna's eyes filled with tears, for she understood what his silence meant. At the sight of her tears his irritation increased.

"Well, what is it?" he asked, looking at her with his dominating coldness.

"Nothing," she said, turning her head away, to hide her emotion.

That question and answer were equivalent to one of the long and stormy discussions that are usual between husbands and wives. Between them such discussions never took place. Their life was regulated according to the compact they had made on that moonlit night at Sorrento; she realised now that what had then seemed to her a way of being saved was only a way of dying more slowly; but he had kept his word, and she must keep hers. He had married her; she must not reproach him. Only sometimes her sorrow appeared too plainly; then he never failed to find a word or a glance to remind her of her promise.

To-day, for the thousandth time, he regretted the sacrifice he had made, and cursed his generosity.

The whole distance from the Toledo to the Campo di Marte was passed in silence. As they approached the Reclusorio, Luigi Caracciolo drove by them with his tandem. He bowed cordially to them. Anna dropped her eyes; Laura smiled upon him.

"What a handsome fellow!" exclaimed Dias, with the sincere admiration of one man of the world for another.

"Very handsome," said Laura, who was accustomed to speak her girlish mind with sufficient freedom.

"He pleases you, eh?" inquired Cesare, with a smile.

"He pleases me," she said, with her habitual freedom and her habitual indifference.

"It's a pity he was never able to take Anna's fancy," Cesare added, with enigmatical irony.

"I hate handsome youths," said Anna, proudly.

"You wouldn't be the impetuous woman that you are, my dear, if you didn't hate everything that other people like. We've got a creature of passion in the family, Laura," he said, with a frank expression of scorn.

"Yes," assented the cruel sister.

Anna smiled faintly in disdain. Again the beauty of the day was extinguished for her; the warm April afternoon was like a dark winter's evening.

The rose that Laura had given her had fallen to pieces, shedding its petals on the carriage floor. Anna would have liked to gather them all up and preserve them. The most she could do, however, was to take a single one that lay in her lap, and put it into the opening of her glove, against the palm of her hand.

At the entrance of the racing-grounds they met the Contessa d'Alemagna again. She smiled graciously upon Anna and Laura. Anna tried to smile in return; Laura bowed coldly.

"Don't you like the Contessa d'Alemagna?" asked Cesare, as he conducted his wife and sister-in-law to their places in the members' stand.

"No," said Laura.

"You're wrong," said he.

"That may be. But she's antipathetic to me."

"I like her," said Anna, feebly.

Cesare found places for them, and gave them each an opera-glass. Then he stood up and said to Anna:

"You will be all right here?"

"Perfectly."

"Nothing I can do for you?"

"Nothing."

"I'll come back for the third race. I'm going now to bet. Good-bye."

And he went off with the light step of a liberated man. Anna watched him as he crossed the turf towards the weighing-stand.

She was surrounded by acquaintances, and they were all talking together. Being a bride, she received a good deal of attention; Dias was popular, and his popularity reflected itself upon her. Besides, people found her interesting, with her black, passionate eyes, the pure oval of her face, and her fresh red lips.

Luigi Caracciolo came up to where the sisters were seated.

"Cesare has deserted you?" he asked, jestingly.

"He's gone to bet. He'll soon come back," said Anna.

"He's betting with the Contessa d'Alemagna," suggested Laura, with one of those perverse smiles which contrasted so oddly with the purity of her face.

"Then he'll not come back so soon," said Luigi, sitting down.

"Have you never seen the races before?" he asked.

"No, I have never seen them," said Anna.

"It's rather a tiresome sight," said he, pulling his blonde moustaches.

"It's interesting to see the people," said Anna.

"It's the crowd that always gives its interest to a scene," said he, with an intonation of profound thought.

Laura was looking through her opera-glass. "There's Cesare," she cried suddenly.

Cesare was walking and talking with the beautiful Contessa d'Alemagna, and two other men, who walked in front of them, occasionally turned and took part in the conversation. As he passed his wife and sister, he looked up and bowed. Anna responded, smiling, but her smile was a forced and weary one.

Luigi Caracciolo, feigning not to have noticed this incident, said to her: "That's a charming dress you're wearing. It's an inspiration."

"Do you like it?" she asked, with a thankful look.

"Yes. I admire these English fashions. I think our women are wrong to go to a horse-race dressed as if for a garden-party. It's not smart."

He took her sunshade and toyed with it, reading the inscription, engraved on its silver handle.

"'*Attendre pour atteindre.*'[A] Is that your motto?" he inquired.

"Yes."

"Have you never had another?"

"Never."

"It's a wise one," he remarked. "It's a fact that everything comes at last to those who know how to wait."

"Alas! not everything, not everything," she murmured, sadly.

There was a burst of applause from the multitude. The second race was over, and the favourite had won, a Naples-bred horse. People crowded about the bookmakers, to receive the value of their bets.

"Perhaps Cesare has won," said Laura. "He was always talking about *Amarilli*."

"Cesare always wins," said Luigi.

"He is not named Cesare[B] for nothing," said Anna, proudly.

"And like the great Julius all his victories were won after he had turned forty—especially those in Germany."[C]

But Anna did not hear this malicious pleasantry. She was thinking of other things.

By and by her husband came to her.

"Are you enjoying it, Anna?" he asked.

"Yes, I am enjoying it."

"And you, Laura?"

"Oh, immensely," she answered, coldly.

"Would you like to see the weighing ground?"

"Yes," she said, taking her shawl and her sunshade.

"I can't take *you*," said Cesare to his wife, who was gazing imploringly at him. "We should look ridiculous."

But she did not appear resigned.

"We should be ridiculous," he repeated imperiously. "Thank goodness, we're not perpetually on our wedding journey."

They went away, leaving her with a pain in her heart which she felt was killing her. She half closed her eyes, and only one idea was clear in the sorrowful confusion of her mind—that her husband was right. She had broken their agreement; she had promised never to entreat him, never to reproach him. It was weak and wicked of her, she told herself, to have consented to such an agreement—a compact by which her love, her pride, and her dignity were alike bound to suffer. She had made another great mistake when she did that, and this time an irreparable mistake.

"Ah, you are alone?" said Luigi Caracciolo, coming up again.

"Alone."

"Something is troubling you. What is it?"

"I am bored; and a person who is bored bores others."

"Let us bore ourselves together, Signora Dias. That will be diverting. I have always wished to bore myself with you, you know."

She shook her head, to forbid his referring to the past.

"Ah, you won't consent? You're very cruel."

She put her opera-glass to her eyes, and looked off across the course.

"If you're going to treat me as badly as this, you'd better send me away," he said, with some feeling.

"The stand is free to all the world," she answered, tormented by the thought that if her husband should come back, he might imagine that she was glad to talk with Caracciolo.

"You are a Domitian in woman's clothes," he cried. "Ah, you women! When you don't like a man you destroy him straightway."

She did not hear him; or, hearing, she did not understand.

"You are too high up for me," he went on. "To descend to my level would be impossible for you and unworthy of you. It's equally impossible for me to rise to yours."

"You are quite mistaken. I'm anything rather than a superior being. I'm a human earthly woman, like all others—more than others."

"Then why do you suffer?"

"Because love is very bitter."

"What love?"

"All love. It is bitterer than aloes, bitterer than gall, bitter in life and in death."

There was another outburst of applause, and the crowd began to move. The races of the first day were over.

Anna looked for her husband. He appeared presently, with Laura on his arm.

"You leave your wife to the most melancholy solitude," said Caracciolo, laughing.

"I was sure you would keep her company, you're such a true friend to me," laughed Cesare.

Caracciolo gave his arm to Anna.

"In any case, it wasn't to render you a service," said Luigi.

"I know your fidelity," said Dias.

"You are my master."

Neither of the ladies spoke. Anna gave herself up to the happiness of having recovered her husband, of going away with him, of taking him home. He seemed excited and pleased, as if he had enjoyed the events of the afternoon without stopping to analyse their frivolity and emptiness. He had amused himself in his usual way, forgetting for the moment the subtle but constant annoyance of his marriage. He was merry, and he showed his merriment by joking with Caracciolo, with Laura, even with his wife.

Anna was very happy. The long day had tired her. But now she felt the warmth and comfort of his presence, and that compensated her for her hours of abandonment. They had some difficulty finding their carriage, but Cesare was not impatient. Caracciolo, meanwhile, was looking for his own tranquilly, never for a moment neglecting his chivalric duties.

When their carriage was discovered, the two men helped the ladies into it; and Cesare, standing beside it, disposed of their shawls and their opera-glasses with the carefulness of a model husband, at the same time exchanging a passing word or two with Caracciolo.

Suddenly Cesare closed the carriage-door, and said to the coachman—"Home."

"Aren't you coming with us?" Anna asked in a low voice.

"No. There's a place for me on Giulio Carafa's four-in-hand. I shall get to Naples sooner than you will. The four-in-hand can go outside the line."

"Four-in-hands are very amusing," said Caracciolo, shaking hands with the two women.

"Shall we have a late dinner?" asked Anna.

"Don't wait dinner for me. I am going to dine at the Contessa d'Alemagna's, with Giulio Carafa and Marco Paliano."

"Very well," said Anna.

She watched Cesare and Luigi as they moved away, puffing their cigarettes. Then she said to the coachman, "Drive home."

During the long drive the sisters scarcely spoke. They were accustomed to respect each other's hours of silence. A soft breeze was blowing from the north. They were both a little pale. Perhaps it was the spectacle of the return from the Campo di Marte, which made them thoughtful; the many carriages, full of people who bore on their faces the signs of happiness due to a fine day of sunshine, passed in the open air, amid the thousand flattering coquetries of love and fancy; the beautiful women, wrapped in their cloaks; the sort of spiritual intoxication that glowed in the eyes of everybody.

The streets were lined by an immense crowd of shop-keepers and working-people, who made a holiday pleasure of watching the stream of carriages; and another crowd looked down from the balconies of the houses.

Presently Anna leaned forward and took her shawl and wrapped it round her shoulders.

"Are you cold?" asked Laura, helping her.

"Yes."

Laura also put on her shawl; she, too, was cold.

Luigi Caracciolo's tandem passed them. Anna did not see him. Laura bowed.

When they had reached the Piazza San Ferdinando, Anna asked: "Would you like to drive about a little?"

"No, let us go home."

And when they were in the house, "We must go in to dinner," Laura said.

"I'm not going to dine. I have a headache," said Anna.

At last she was alone. In her own room she threw aside her hat and veil, her sunshade, her purse, her pocket-handkerchief; she fell into an arm-chair, and was shaken by a storm of sobs and tears.

From above her little writing-table Cesare's portrait seemed to smile upon the flowers that were placed under it.

She raised her eyes, and looked at his beautiful and noble face, which appeared to glow with love and life. A great impulse of passion rose in her heart; she took the portrait and kissed it, and bathed it in her tears, murmuring, "my love, my love, why do you treat me like this? Ah, I can only love you, love you; and you are killing me."

Hours passed unnoticed by her. Some one came to her door and asked whether she wished for a lamp; she answered, "No."

By-and-bye she saw a white figure standing before her. She recognised Laura. And she saw that Laura was weeping. She had never seen her weep before.

"You are crying. What are you crying for?" she asked.

"Yes," answered Laura, vaguely, with a gesture.

And they wept together.

FOOTNOTES:

[A] "Wait to win." In French in the original.

[B] Cæsar.

[C] Alemagna. A punning reference to the Contessa.

II.

Cesare Dias came home one day towards six o'clock, in great good humour. At dinner he found everything excellent, though it was his habit to find everything bad. He ate with a hearty appetite, and told countless amusing stories, of the sort that he reserved for his agreeable moments. He joked with Laura, and with Anna; he even complimented his wife upon her dress, a new one that she had to-day put on for the first time. He succeeded in communicating his gaiety to the two women. Anna looked at him with meek and tender eyes; and as often as he smiled she smiled too.

Laura, it is true, spoke little, but in her face shone that expression of vivacity, of animation, which had characterised it for some time past. She agreed with everything Cesare said, bowing her head.

After dinner they all passed into Anna's drawing-room. It was her evening at home; and noticing that there were flowers in all the vases—it was in June, just a year after their talk at Sorrento—and seeing the silver samovar on the table, Cesare asked: "Are you expecting people to-night, Anna?"

"A few. Perhaps no one will come."

"Ah, that's why you've got yourself up so smartly."

"Did you fancy it was for you, that she had put on her new frock, Cesare?" Laura asked, jestingly.

"I was presumptuous enough to do so; and all presumptions are delusions. I'll bet that Luigi Caracciolo is coming—the ever faithful one."

"I'm sure I don't know," said Anna, indifferently.

"Oh, you hypocrite, Anna!" laughed Laura.

"Hypocrite, hypocrite!" repeated Cesare, also laughing. "Come, I'll warrant that the obstinate fidelity of Caracciolo has at last made an impression. Admirable! He's been in love with you for a hundred years."

"Oh, Cesare, don't joke about such subjects," Anna begged, in pain.

"You see, Laura, she is troubled."

"She's troubled, it's true," affirmed Laura.

"You're both of you heartless," Anna murmured.

Cesare opened his cigarette case, and playfully offered a cigarette to each of the ladies.

"I don't smoke," said Laura.

"Why don't you learn to?"

"Smoke is bad for the teeth;" and she showed her own, shining like those of Beatrice in the tale by Edgar Poe.

"You're right, fair Minerva. Will you smoke, Anna?"

"I don't smoke, either," she said, with a soft smile.

"You ought to learn. It would be becoming to you. You're dark, you have the Spanish type, and a *papelito*[D] would complete your charm."

"I will learn, Cesare," she assented.

"And what's more, smoke calms the nerves. You can't imagine the soothing effect it has. Nothing is better to relieve our little sorrows."

"Give me a cigarette, then," she said at once.

"Ah, you have little sorrows?"

"Who knows!" she sighed, putting aside her cigarette.

"You have no little sorrows, Laura?" asked Cesare.

"Neither little ones nor big ones."

"Who can boast of having never wept?" said Anna, with a melancholy accent.

"If we become sentimental, I shall take myself off," said Cesare.

"No, no, don't go away," Anna prayed him.

"I would remind you that we've got to pass our whole life-time together," said he, ironically, knocking off the ash of his cigarette.

"All our life-time, and more beyond it," said Anna, pensively.

"And more beyond! It's a grave affair. I will think of it while I am dressing, this evening."

"Where are you going?"

"To take a walk," he answered, rising.

"Why don't you stay here?" she ventured to ask.

"I can't. I'm obliged to go out."

"Come home early, won't you?"

"Early—yes," he consented, after a short hesitation.

"I'll wait for you, Cesare."

"Yes, yes. Good-night."

He went off.

Laura, according to her recent habit, had listened to this dialogue with her eyes half closed, and biting her lips; she said nothing. Whenever her sister and her brother-in-law exchanged a few affectionate words (and, indeed, Cesare did no more than respond to the affection of Anna), she assumed the countenance of a statue, which neither feels nor hears nor sees; or else, she got up and left the room noiselessly. Often Anna surprised on Laura's face a cynical smile that appeared the antithesis of its extreme purity, the irony of an icy virgin who is aware of the falsity and hollowness of love.

This evening, when Cesare had left them, the sisters remained together for a few minutes. But apparently both their minds were absorbed in deep thought; at any rate they could not keep up a conversation. Anna, in her lilac-coloured frock, lay in an easy-chair, leaning her head on her hands, over which her black hair seemed like a warrior's helmet. Laura was pulling and playing with the fringe of her white dress.

"I'm going; good night," she said suddenly.

"Why do you go, Laura?" asked Anna, issuing from her reverie.

"There's no use staying. People will be arriving."

"But stay for that very reason. You will help me to endure their visits."

"Oh, that's a task above my strength," said the blonde and beautiful Minerva. "Then, anyhow, it's you they come to see, my dear."

"You'll be married some day yourself," said Anna, laughing.

She was still in a pleasant mood—a reflection of Cesare's gaiety; and then he had promised to come home early.

"Who knows! Good night," and Laura rose to go away.

"But what are you going to do?"

"Read a little; then sleep."

"What are you reading?"

"'*Le mot de l'énigme*,'[E] by Madame Pauline Craven."

"A mystical romance? Do you want to become a nun?"

"Who knows! Good night."

Anna herself took up a book after Laura's departure. It was *Adolphe*, by Benjamin Constant; she had found it one day on her husband's writing-desk. In its cool yet ardent pages one feels the charm of a truthful story, surging up from the heart in a single, vibrant cry of pain. Anna had read it two or three times; now she began it again, absent-mindedly. But she did not read long. A few callers came; the Marchesa Scibilia, her relative, accompanied by Gaetano Althan, who always liked to go about with old ladies; Commander Gabriele Mari, a man of seventy; and then the Prince of Gioiosa, a handsome, witty, and intelligent Calabrian.

The conversation, of course, was a mixture of frivolity and seriousness, as conversations are apt to be in a small gathering like the present, where nobody cares to appear too much in earnest, and everybody tries to speak in paradoxes.

The Prince di Gioiosa was the last to leave; it was then past eleven.

"No one else will come," she thought.

But she was mistaken. Acquaintances passing in the street, and seeing her windows alight, came up to pay their respects. When the last of these had gone, "It is late; no one else will come," she thought again.

But again she was mistaken. The servant announced Luigi Caracciolo; and the handsome young fellow entered, with that English correctness of bearing which somewhat tempered the vivacity of his blonde youthfulness. He was in evening dress, and wore a spray of lilies of the valley in his button-hole.

Anna gave him her hand amicably. Her rings glittered in the lamplight.

"Starry hand," he said, bowing, and pressing it softly.

"Where do you come from?" she asked, with that polite curiosity which implies no real interest.

"From the opera," he said, seating himself beside her.

"What were they giving?"

"'The Huguenots'—always the same."

"It is always beautiful."

"Do you remember?" he asked with a tender, caressing voice. "They were singing 'The Huguenots' on the evening when I was introduced to you."

"Yes, yes; I remember that evening," she said, with sudden melancholy.

"How horribly I displeased you that night, didn't I? The only thing to approach it was the tremendously delightful impression you made on me."

"What nonsense!" she protested kindly.

"And your first impression of me has never changed—confess it," he said.

"Even if that were true, it wouldn't make you very unhappy."

"What can you know about that? You beautiful women, admired and loved—what do you know?"

"You're right. Indeed, we know nothing."

But he saw that her mind was away in a land of dreams, far from him. He felt all at once the distance that divided them.

"When you come back from your travels let me know, that I may welcome you," he said, with his smooth, caressing voice.

"What travels?"

"Ah! If I knew! If I knew where your thoughts are wandering while I talk to you, I could go with you, I could follow you in your fantasies. Instead, I speak, and you don't listen to me. I say serious things to you in a jesting tone, and you understand neither the seriousness nor the joke. You leave me here alone, whilst you roam—who knows where? And I, a humble mortal, without visions, without imagination, I can only wait for your return, my dear lady."

If, indeed, there was a certain poetic quality in what he said, there was a deeper poetry still in the tenderness and sweetness of his voice. He sat in front of her, gazing into her face, as if he could not tear himself from that contemplation. She sometimes lowered her eyes, sometimes turned them away, sometimes fixed them upon a page of *Adolphe*, which she had kept in her hands. If his gaze embarrassed her, however, his soft voice seemed to calm her nerves. She listened to it, scarcely understanding his words, as one listens to a vague pleasant music.

"Doesn't it bore you to wait?" she asked.

"I am never bored here. When I have this lovely sight before my eyes."

"What sight?" she inquired, ingenuously.

"Your person, my dear lady."

"But you can't always be looking at me," she said, laughing, trying to turn the conversation to a jest.

"That's a fatal misfortune, as they say in novels. I should like to pass my whole life near to you. Instead, I'm obliged to pass it among a lot of people who are utterly indifferent to me. A great misfortune!"

"It's not your fault," she said, with a faint smile.

"It certainly isn't. But that doesn't console me. Shall we try it—passing our lives together? One can overcome misfortunes. Our whole lives—that will mean many years."

"But I am married," she said, feeling that the talk was becoming dangerous.

"Oh, that's nothing," he cried emphatically.

"Caracciolo, I believe you've found the means to see me no more. What do you want from me?"

"Nothing, dear lady, nothing," he answered, with genuine grief in his face and voice.

"Then you ought not to risk destroying one of your friendships. What would Cesare have said if he had heard you for the last half hour?"

"Oh, nothing. He couldn't have heard me, you know, because he's never here."

"Sometimes he is," she said, with sudden emotion.

"Never, never. Don't tell pious fibs."

"He's always here."

"In your heart. I know it. It's an agreeable home for him, the more so because he can find others of the same sort wherever he goes."

"What are you saying?"

"One of my usual vulgarities. I'm speaking ill of your husband."

"Then be quiet."

But to soften the severity of this command, she offered him a box of cigarettes.

"Thanks for your charity," he said.

And he began to smoke, looking at one of her slippers of lilac satin embroidered with silver, which escaped from beneath her train. She sat with her elbow on the table, thinking. It was midnight. In a few minutes Caracciolo would be gone; and Cesare couldn't delay much longer about coming home.

Luigi Caracciolo seemed to divine her thoughts.

"After this cigarette, I will leave you. I'm afraid I've given you no great idea of my wit."

"I detest witty men."

"Small harm! I hope you believe, though, that I have a heart."

"I believe it."

"All the better. One day or another you will remember what I have said to you this evening, and understand it."

"Perhaps," she said, vaguely.

"You had a very happy inspiration, to dress in lilac. It's such a tender colour. That's the tint one sees in the sunsets at Venice. Have you ever been at Venice?"

"Never."

"That's a pity. It's a place full of soft tears. One can make a provision of them there, to last a life-time. Trifling loves become deep at Venice, and deep loves become indestructible. Good-night."

"Good-night."

She gave him her hand, like a white flower issuing from the satin of her sleeve. He touched it lightly with his lips, and went away.

Not for a moment during her conversation with Luigi Caracciolo had her husband been absent from Anna's mind. And all that the young man said, which constantly implied if it did not directly mention love, had but intensified her one eternal thought.

It was now half-past twelve. She rose and rang the bell; and her maid appeared.

They left the drawing-room and went into Anna's bedroom, which was lighted by a big lamp with a shade of pink silk.

Her maid helped her to undress, thinking that she was going to bed; but presently Anna asked for her tea-gown of cream-coloured crape, and put it on, as if she meant to sit up. She had loosened her hair, and it fell down her back in a single rich black tress.

The maid asked if she might go to bed. Anna said, "Yes." Cesare had given orders that no servant should ever sit up for him; he had a curiously wrought little key, a master-key, which he wore on his watch-chain, and which opened every door in his house. Thus he could come in at any hour of the night he liked, without being seen or heard. The maid went softly away, closing the door behind her.

Anna sat down in an easy chair, beside her bed. She still had the volume of *Adolphe* in her hand. She sat still there, while she heard the servant moving about the apartment, shutting the windows. Then all was silent.

Anna got up, and opened the doors between her room and her husband's. So she would be able to hear him when he returned. He could not delay much longer. He had promised her to come home early; he knew that she would wait for him. And, as she had been doing through the whole evening, but with greater intensity than ever, she longed for the presence of her loved one. Was not every thing empty and colourless when he was away? And this evening he had been so merry and so kind. His promise resounded in her soul like a solemn vow. She thrilled with tremulous emotion. The softness of the spring night entered into her and exhilarated her.

She lay back in her easy-chair, with closed eyes, and dreamed of his coming. She felt an immense need of him, to have him there beside her, to hold his hand in hers, to lean her head upon his shoulder in sweet, deep peace, listening to the beating of his heart, supported by his arms, while his breath fell upon her hair, her eyelids, her lips. A dream of love; vivid and languid, full of delicate ardour and melancholy desire.

She surprised herself murmuring his name. "Cesare, Cesare," she said, trembling with love at the sound of her own voice.

Suddenly it seemed to her that she heard a noise in her husband's room. Then he had come!

Swiftly, like a flying shadow, she crossed the passage, and looked in. Only silence and darkness! She had been mistaken. She leaned on the frame of the door, and remained thus for a long moment.

Slowly she returned to her own room, thinking that "early" must mean for a man of late habits like Cesare two o'clock in the morning. That was it! He would arrive at two.

She took up *Adolphe*, thinking to divert herself with reading, and thus to moderate her impatience. She opened the book towards the middle, where the passionate struggle between Ellenore and Adolphe is shown in all its sorrowful intensity. And from the dry, precise words, the hard, effective style, the brief and austere narrative, which was like the cry of a soul destroyed by scepticism, Anna derived an impression of fright. Ah, in her sincere, youthful faith, what a horror she had of that modern malady which corrupts the mind, depraves the conscience, and kills whatever is most noble in the soul! What could she know, poor, simple, ignorant woman, whose only belief, whose only law, whose only hope was love—what could she know of the spiritual diseases of those who have seen too much, who have loved too much, who have squandered the purest treasures of their feelings? What could she know of the desolating torture of those souls who can no longer believe in anything, not even in themselves, and who have lost their last ideal? She could know nothing; and yet a terror assailed her. Perhaps Cesare, her husband, was like *Adolphe*, who could never more be happy, who could never more give happiness to others. She shuddered, and threw the book aside, in great distress.

She got up mechanically, and took from a table a rosary of sandal wood, which a Missionary Friar had brought from Jerusalem.

She had never been regular in her devotions; her imagination was too fervid. But religious feelings seemed sometimes to sweep in upon her in great waves of divine love. A child of the South, she only prayed when moved by some strong pain, for which she could find no earthly relief. She forgot to pray when she was happy. Now she pressed her rosary to her lips, and began to repeat the long and poetical Litany, which Domenico de Guzman has dedicated to the Virgin. Ingenuously enough, she thought that in this way the time would pass more rapidly, two o'clock would strike, and Cesare would arrive. But she endeavoured in vain to fix her mind upon her orisons; it flew away, before her, to her meeting with her Beloved; and though her lips pronounced the words of the *Ave* and the *Pater*, their sense escaped her. Once or twice she paused for a few minutes, and then went on, confused, beseeching Heaven's pardon for her slight attention.

When her rosary was finished, it was two precisely. Now Cesare would come.

She could not control her nervousness. She took her lamp and went into her husband's room: she placed the lamp on the writing-desk, and seated herself in one of the leather arm-chairs. She felt easier here; the austerity of the big chamber, with its dark furniture, told her that her husband's soul was above the sterile and frivolous pleasures in which he had already lost the best part of the night.

The air still smelt of cigarette smoke. Here and there a point of metal gleamed in the lamplight. On a table lay a pair of gloves; they had been worn that day, and they retained the form of his hands. She kissed them, and put them into the bosom of her gown.

But where was Cesare?

She began to pace backwards and forwards, the train of her dress following her like a white wave. Why did he not come home? It was late, very late. There were no balls on for that night; no social function could detain him till this hour.

Where was Cesare? Ah, Cesare, Cesare, Cesare, her dear love, where was he? She passed her hands over her burning forehead.

All at once, looking out into the night, she noticed in the distance the windows of Cesare's club, brilliantly lighted. Then a sudden peace came to her. He would be there, playing, talking, enjoying the company of his friends, forgetful of the time. It was an old habit of his, and old habits are so hard to break. She remained at the window of his room, with her eyes fixed upon the windows of his club; the light that shone from them was the pole-star of her heart.

She opened the window and went out upon the balcony.

Presently two men issued from the club-house, stood for a moment chatting together at the entrance, and then moved off towards the Chiaia. Ah, she thought, the company at the Club was beginning to break up; at last Cesare would come. At the end of ten minutes, four men came out together. These also chatted together for a minute, then separated, two going towards the Riviera, two entering the Via Vittoria. By-and-by one man came out alone, and advanced directly towards Dias' house. This, this surely would be he.

The man was looking up, towards the balcony.

"Good-night, Signora Anna," said the voice of Luigi Caracciolo.

"Good-night," she murmured, faint with disappointment.

Caracciolo had stopped, and was leaning on the railing, gazing up at her. Anna drew back out of sight.

"Good-night, Anna," he repeated, very softly.

She did not answer.

Caracciolo went off, slowly, slowly; stopping now and then to look back.

She turned her eyes again upon the windows of the club, but they were quite dark; the lights had been extinguished.

So Caracciolo had been the last to leave; and Cesare was not there!

She felt terribly cold, all at once. Her teeth chattered. She went back into the room, shivering, and had scarcely strength enough to shut the window. She fell upon a chair, exhausted. The clock struck. It was half-past three.

And now a hideous suspicion began to torture her. There were no balls to-night, no receptions, no functions. The club was shut up. The cafés were shut up. All talking, eating, drinking, gambling, were over for the night. The life of the night was spent. Everybody had gone home to bed. Then where was Cesare? Cesare, her husband, was with a woman! And jealousy began to gnaw her heart. With a woman; that was certain. The truth burned her soul. He could be nowhere else than with a woman. The truth rang in her heart like a trumpet-blast. Mechanically she put her fingers to her ears to shut out the words—*with a woman, with a woman.*

But what woman?

She knew nothing of her husband's secrets, nothing of his past or present loves.

She was a mere stranger whom he tolerated, not a friend, not a confidant. She was a troublesome bond upon him, an obstacle to his pleasures, an interference with his habits. No doubt there were older bonds, stronger ties, that kept him from her; or it might be the mere force of a passing fancy. But for what woman, for what woman? In vain she tried to give the woman a name, a living form.

Oh, certainly not a lady, not a woman of honourable rank and reputation; not the Contessa d'Alemagna.

Who then? Who then?

How much time passed, while she sat there, in a convulsion of tears and sobs, prey to all the anguish of jealousy?

The day broke; a greenish, livid light entered the room.

The handle of the door turned. Cesare came in. He was very pale, with dull, weary eyes. He had a cigarette in his mouth; his lips were blue. The collar of his overcoat was turned up; his hands were in his pockets. He looked at his wife indifferently, coldly, as if he did not recognise her.

She rose. Her face was ashen. Her capacity for feeling was exhausted.

"What are you doing here?" he asked.

He threw away his cigarette, and took off his hat. How old and used up he looked, with his hair in disorder, his cheeks sunken from lack of sleep.

"I was waiting for you," she said.

"All night?"

"All night."

"You have great patience."

He opened the door.

"Good-bye, Anna."

"Good-bye, Cesare."

And she returned to her own room.

FOOTNOTES:

[D] Spanish in the original.

[E] The key to the riddle.

III.

About the middle of June, in the first summer of his marriage, Cesare Dias brought his wife and his sister-in-law to the Villa Caterina at Sorrento. He would leave them there, while he went to take the baths at Vichy. Afterwards he was going to Saint-Moritz in the Engadine, whither betake themselves such persons as desire to be cold in summer, the same who, desiring to be hot in winter, hibernate at Nice. Anna had secretly wished to accompany her husband upon this journey, longing to be alone with him, far from their usual surroundings; but she was to be left behind.

Ever since that night when she had sat up till dawn waiting for him, tormented, disillusioned, her faith destroyed, her moral strength exhausted, there had been a coldness between the couple. Cesare had lost no time in asserting his independence of her, and had vouchsafed but the vaguest explanations, saying in general terms that a man might pass a night out of his house, chatting with friends or playing cards, for any one of a multitude of reasons. Anna had listened without answering. She dreaded above all things having a quarrel with her husband. She closed her eyes and listened. He flung his explanation at her with an air of contempt. She was silent but not satisfied.

She could never forget the hours of that night, when, for the first time, she had drained her cup of bitterness to its dregs, and looked into the bottom depths of human wickedness. The sweetness of her love had then been poisoned.

As for Cesare, he had been exceedingly annoyed by her waiting for him, which seemed to him an altogether extravagant manifestation of her fondness. It annoyed him to have been surprised in the early morning light looking old and ugly; it annoyed him to have to explain his absence; and it annoyed him finally to think that similar scenes might occur again. Oh, how he loathed these tragic women and their tragedies! After having hated them his whole life long, them and their tears and their vapourings, behold! he had been trapped into marrying one of them—for his sins; and his rancour at the inconceivable folly he had committed vented itself upon Anna. She, sad in the essence of her soul, humble, disheartened, understood her husband's feelings; and by means of her devotion and tenderness sought to procure his pardon for her offence—the offence of having waited for him that night! One day, when Anna had been even more penitent and more affectionate than usual, he had indeed made some show of forgiving her, with the pretentious indulgence of a superior being; she had taken his forgiveness as a slave takes a kind word after a beating, smiling with tears in her eyes, happy that he had not punished her more heavily for her fault.

But the truth is, he was a man and not an angel. He had forgiven her; yet he still wished to punish her. On no consideration would he take her with him to Vichy and Saint-Moritz. He gave her to understand that their wedding-journey was finished; that it would never do to leave her sister Laura alone for two months with no other chaperone than Stella Martini; that it wasn't his wish to play Joseph Prudhomme, and travel in the bosom of his family; in short, he gave her to understand in a thousand ways that he wished to go alone; and she resigned herself to staying behind in preference to forcing her company upon him. She flattered herself, poor thing, that this act of submission, so hard for her to make, would restore her to her lord's good graces. He went away, indeed in great good temper. He seemed rejuvenated. The idea of the absolute liberty he was about to enjoy filled him with enthusiasm. He recommended his ladies (as he jokingly called the sisters) not to be too nun-like, but to go out, to receive, to amuse themselves as they wished. Anna heard this advice, pale with downcast eyes; Laura listened to it with an odd smile on her lips, looking straight into her brother-in-law's face. She too was pale and mute.

After his departure a great, sad silence seemed to invade the villa. Each of the sisters was pensive and reserved; they spoke but little together; they even appeared to avoid each other. For the rest, the charming youthful serenity of the blonde Minerva had vanished; her white brow was clouded with thought. They were in the same house, but for some time they rarely met.

Anna wrote to Cesare twice a day; she told him everything that happened; she opened to him her every fancy, her every dream; she wrote with the effusiveness of a passionate woman, who, too timid to express herself by spoken words, finds her outlet in letters. Writing, she could tell him how she loved him, that she was his in body and soul. Cesare wrote to her once or twice a week, and not at length; but in each of his notes there would be, if not a word of love, at least some kindly phrase; and upon that Anna would live for three or four days—until his next letter arrived. He was enjoying himself; he was feeling better; he would return soon. Sometimes he even expressed a wish for her presence, that she might share his pleasure in a landscape or laugh with him at some original fellow-traveller. He always sent his remembrances to Laura; and Anna would read them out to her.

"Thank you," was all that Laura responded.

Laura herself wrote a good deal in these days. What was she writing? And to whom? She sat at her little desk, shut up in her room, and covered big sheets of paper with her clear, firm handwriting. If any one entered, she covered what she had written with her blotting-paper, and remained silent, with lowered eyes, toying with her pen. More than once Anna had come in. Thereupon Laura had gathered up her manuscripts, and locked them into a drawer, controlling with an effort the trouble in her face.

"What are you writing?" Anna asked one day, overcoming her timidity, and moved by a strange impulse of curiosity.

"Nothing that would interest you," the other answered.

"How can you say so?" the elder sister protested, with indulgent tenderness. "Whatever pleases you or moves you must interest me."

"Nothing pleases me and nothing moves me," Laura said, looking down.

"Not even what you are writing?"

"Not even what I am writing."

"How reserved you are! How close you keep your secrets! But why should you have any?" Anna insisted affectionately.

"Yes," said Laura, vaguely. She got up and left the room, carrying her key with her.

Anna never again referred to what her sister was writing. It might be letters, it might be a journal.

In July, Sorrento filled up with tourists and holiday folk; and the other villas were occupied by their owners. The sisters were invited about a good deal, and lured into the thousand summer gaieties of the town.

One of the earliest arrivals was Luigi Caracciolo. He came to Sorrento every season, but usually not till the middle of August, and then to spend no more than a fortnight. He had rather a disdain for Sorrento, he who had travelled over the whole of Europe. This year he came in the first week of July; and he was determined to stay until Anna Dias left. He was genuinely in love with her; in his own way, of course. The mystery that hung over her past, and her love for Cesare Dias, which Luigi knew to be unrequited, made her all the dearer to him. He was in love, as men are in love who have loved many times before. Sometimes he lost his head a little in her presence, but never more than a little. He retained his mastery of himself sufficiently to pursue his own well-proved methods of love-making. He covered his real passion with a semblance of levity which served admirably to compel Anna to tolerate it.

She never allowed him—especially at Sorrento, where she was alone and where she was very sad—to speak of love; but she could not forbid him to call occasionally at the Villa Caterina, nor could she help meeting him here and there in the town. And Cesare, from Saint-Moritz, kept writing to her and Laura to amuse themselves, to go out, saying that he hated women who lived like recluses. And sometimes he would add a joking message for Caracciolo, calling him Anna's faithful cavalier; but she, through delicacy, had not delivered them.

Luigi did not pay too open a court to her, did not affect too great an intimacy; but he was never far from her. For a whole evening he would hover near her at a party, waiting for the moment when he might seat himself beside her; he would leave when she left, and on the pretext of taking a little walk in the moonlight, would accompany the two ladies to the door of their house. He was persevering, with a gentle, continuous, untiring perseverance that nothing could overcome, neither Anna's silence, nor her coldness, nor her melancholy. She often spoke to him of Cesare, and with so much feeling in her voice that he turned pale, wounded in his pride, disappointed in his desire, yet not despairing, for it is always a hopeful sign when a woman loves, even though she loves another. Then the only difficulty (though an immense one) is to change the face of the man she loves to your own, by a sort of sentimental sleight of hand.

For various reasons, he was extremely cautious. He was not one of those who enjoy advertising their desires and their discomfitures on the walls of the town. Then, he did not wish to alarm Anna, and cause her to close her door to him. And besides, he was afraid of the silent watchfulness of Laura. The beautiful Minerva and the handsome young man had never understood each other; they were given to exchanging somewhat sharp words at their encounters, a remarkable proceeding on the part of Laura, who usually talked little, and then only in brief and colourless sentences. Her contempt for him was undisguised. It appeared in her manner of looking him over when he wore a new suit of clothes, in her manner of beginning and ending her remarks to him with the phrase, "A handsome young fellow like you." That was rather bold, for a girl, but Laura was over twenty, and both the sisters passed for being nice, but rather original, nice but original, as their mother and father had been before them. Luigi Caracciolo himself thought them odd, but the oddity of Anna was adorable, that of Laura made him uneasy and distrustful. He was afraid that on one day or another, she might denounce him to Cesare, and betray his love for the other's wife. She had such a sarcastic smile sometimes on her lips! And her laughter had such a scornful ring! He imagined the most fantastic things in respect of her, and feared her mightily.

"How strange your sister is," he said once to Anna, finding her alone.

"She's good, though," said Anna, thoughtfully.

"Does she seem so to you?"

"Yes."

"You little know. You're very ingenuous. She's probably a monster of perfidy," he said softly.

"Why do you say that to me, Caracciolo? Don't you know that I dislike such jokes?"

"If I offend you, I'll hold my tongue. I keep my opinion, though. Some day you'll agree with me."

"Be quiet, Caracciolo. You distress me."

"It's much better to have no illusions; then we can't lose them, dear lady."

"It is better to lose illusions, than never to have had them."

"What a deep heart is yours! How I should like to drown in it! Let me drown myself in your heart, Anna."

"Don't call me by my name," she said, as if she had heard only his last word.

"I will obey," he answered meekly.

"You, too, are good," she murmured, absently.

"I am as bad as can be, Signora," he rejoined, piqued.

She shook her head good-naturedly, with the smile of one who would not believe in human wickedness, who would keep her faith intact, in spite of past delusions. And the more Luigi Caracciolo posed as a depraved character, the more she showed her belief that at the bottom every human soul is good.

"Everybody is good, according to you," he said. "Then I suppose your husband, Cesare, is good too?"

"Too? He is the best of all. He is absolutely good," she cried, her voice softening as it always did when she spoke of Cesare.

"He who leaves you here alone after a few months of marriage?"

"But I'm not alone," she retorted, simply.

"You're not alone—you're in bad company," he said, nervously.

"Do you think so? I wasn't aware of it."

"You couldn't tell me more politely that I'm a nonentity. But he, he who is away, and who no doubt invents a thousands pretence to explain his absence to you—can you really say that he is good."

"Cesare invents no pretences for me," she replied, turning pale.

"Who says so? He? Do you believe him?"

"He says nothing. I have faith in him," she answered, overwhelmed to hear her own daily fears thus uttered for her.

Caracciolo looked at her anxiously. Merely to hear her pronounce her husband's name proved that she adored him. Luigi was too expert a student of women not to interpret rightly her pallor, her emotion, her distress. He did not know, but he could easily guess that Anna wrote to Cesare every day, and that he responded rarely and briefly. He understood how heavy her long hours of solitude must be, amid the blue and green of the Sorrento landscape, passed in constant longing for her husband's presence. He understood perfectly that she was consumed by secret jealousy, and that he tortured her cruelly when by a word, or an insinuation he inspired her with new suspicions. He could read her heart like an open book; but he loved her all the better for the intense passion that breathed from its pages. He did not despair. Sooner or later, he was convinced, he would succeed in overcoming the obstacle in his way. He adopted the ancient method of assailing the character of the absent man.

When he would mention some old flame of Cesare's, or some affair that still continued, and which his marriage could not break off, or when he would speak of Cesare's desertion of his young wife, he saw Anna's face change; he knew the anguish that he woke in her heart, and he suffered wretchedly to realise that it was for the love of another man. His weapon was a double-edged sword, that wounded her and wounded him. But what of that? He continued to wield it, believing that thus little by little he could deface the image of Cesare Dias that Anna consecrated with her adoration.

Anna was always ready to talk of her husband, and that gave him his opportunity for putting in his innuendoes. At the same time it caused him much bitterness of spirit, and sometimes he would say, "We are three. How do you do, Cesare?" bowing to an imaginary presence.

Anna's eyes filled with tears at such moments.

"Forgive me, forgive me," he cried. "But when you introduce his name into our conversation, you cause me such agony that I feel I am winning my place in heaven. Go on: I am already tied to the rack; force your knife into my heart, gentle torturess."

And she, at first timidly, but then with the impetuousness of an open and generous nature, would continue to talk of Cesare. Where was he, what was he doing, when would he return? she would ask; and he by-and-by would interrupt her speculations to suggest that Cesare was probably just now on the Righi, with the Comtesse de Béhague, one of his old French loves, whom he met every year in Switzerland; and that he would very likely not return to Sorrento at all, nor even to Naples before the end of October.

"I don't believe it, I don't believe it," she protested.

"You don't believe it? But it's his usual habit. Why should he alter it this year?"

"He has me to think of now."

"Ah, dear Anna, dear Anna, he thinks of you so little!"

"Don't call me by my name," she said, making a gesture to forbid him.

"If Cesare heard me he wouldn't like it—eh?"

"I think so."

"You hope so, dear lady, which is a very different thing. But he's not jealous."

"No; he's not jealous," she repeated, softly, lost in sorrowful meditations. "But what man is?"

"He's a man who has never thought of anything but his own pleasure."

"Sad, sad," she murmured very low.

Yet, though she thoroughly well understood that a better knowledge of her husband's past life could only bring her greater pain, she began to question Luigi Caracciolo about Cesare's adventures. Ah, how ashamed she was to do so! It seemed like violating a confidence; like desecrating an idol that she had erected on the altar of her heart. It seemed like breaking the most sacred condition of love, which is secrecy, to speak thus of her love to a man who loved her. Yet the temptation was too strong for her. And cautiously, by hints, she endeavoured to draw from Caracciolo some fact, some episode, a detail, a name, a date; she would try to ask indifferently, feigning a slight interest, attempting without success to play the woman of wit—she, poor thing, who was only a woman of heart.

Caracciolo understood at once, and for form's sake assumed a certain reluctance. Then, as if won by her wishes, he would speak; he would give her a fact, an episode, a date, a name, commenting upon it in such wise as, without directly speaking ill of Cesare, to underline his hardness of heart and his incapacity for real passion. It was sad wisdom that Anna hereby gained. Her husband's soul was cold and arid; he had always been the same; nothing had ever changed him. Sometimes, sick and tired, she would pray Caracciolo by a gesture to stop his talk; she would remain thoughtful and silent, feeling that she had poured a corrosive acid into her own wounds. Sometimes Laura would be present at these conversations, beautiful, in white garments, with soft, lovely eyes. She listened to Caracciolo with close attention, whilst an inscrutable smile played on her virginal lips. He, in deference to the young girl's presence, would, from time to time, drop the subject; then Laura would look at him with an expression of ardent curiosity that surprised him, a look that seemed to ask a hundred questions. His narrative of the life of Cesare Dias succeeded in spoiling Anna's holiday, but did not advance his courtship by an inch.

He has great patience, and unlimited faith in his method. He knew that a strong passion or a strong desire can overcome in time the most insurmountable obstacles. Yet he had moments of terrible discouragement. How she loved him, Cesare Dias, this beautiful woman! It was a love all the more sad to contemplate, because of the discrepancies of age and character between husband and wife. Here was a fresh young girl uncomplainingly supporting the neglect of a worn-out man of forty.

One day, unexpectedly, Cesare returned. From his wife's pallor, from her trembling, he understood how much he had been loved during his absence. He was very kind to her, very gallant, very tender. He embraced her and kissed her many times, effusively, and told her that she was far lovelier than the ladies of France and Switzerland. He was in the best of good humours; and she, laughing with tears in her eyes, and holding his hand as she stood beside him, realised anew how single and absolute was her love for him.

Two or three times Cesare asked, "And Laura?"

"She's very well. She'll be coming soon."

"You haven't found her a husband?"

"She doesn't want one."

"That's what all girls say."

"Laura is obstinate. She really doesn't want one. People even think she would like to become a nun."

"Nonsense."

"The strange thing is that once when I asked her if it was true, she answered no."

"She's an odd girl," said Cesare, a little pensively.

"I don't understand her."

"Ah, for that matter, you understand very little in general," said her husband, caressing her hair to temper his impertinence.

"Oh, you're right; very little," she answered, with a happy smile. "I'm an imbecile."

But Laura did not come, though she had been called. Anna sent her maid. "She would come at once; she was dressing," was the reply. They waited for her a few minutes longer; and when she appeared in the doorway, dazzling in white, with her golden hair in a rich coil on the top of her head, Anna cried, "Laura, Cesare has come."

Cesare rose and advanced to meet his sister-in-law. She gave him her hand, and he kissed it. But he saw that she was offering her face; then he embraced her, kissing her cheek, which was like the petal of a camellia. This was all over in an instant, but it seemed a long instant to Anna; and she had an instinctive feeling of repulsion when Laura, blushing a little, came up and kissed her. It was an instinctive caress on the part of Laura, and an instinctive movement of repulsion on that of Anna. Not that she had the faintest evil thought or suspicion; it was a vague distress, a subtle pain, nothing else.

From that day life in the quiet Villa Caterina became sensibly gayer; there were visits and receptions, dances, and yachting parties. It was an extremely lively season at Sorrento. There were a good many foreigners in the town; amongst them two or three wild American girls, who swam, rowed, played croquet and lawn-tennis, were very charming, and had handsome dowries. It became the fashion for the men to make love to these young persons, a thing that was sufficiently unusual in a society where flirtation with unmarried women is supposed to be forbidden. Cesare told Anna that it was a propitious moment for launching Laura; she too had a handsome dowry, and was very lovely, though she lacked perhaps the vivacity of the wild Americans; and with the energy of a youth, he took his wife and sister everywhere.

Luigi Caracciolo continued to make his court to Anna. With delicate cynicism, Cesare, on his return, had inquired whether Luigi had faithfully discharged his duty as her cavalier, but Anna had turned such talk aside, for it hurt her. Laura, however, declared that Luigi had accomplished miracles of devotion, and shown himself a model of constancy.

"And the lady, what of her?" asked Cesare, pulling his handsome black moustaches.

"Heartless," Laura answered, smiling at Anna, for whom this joking was a martyrdom.

"Noble but heartless lady!" repeated Cesare.

"Would you have wished me to be otherwise?" demanded Anna, quickly, looking into her husband's eyes.

"No; I should not have wished it," was his prompt rejoinder.

In spite of this downright pronouncement, in which her husband, for all his cynicism, asserted his invincible right to her fidelity—in spite of the fact that Cesare appeared to watch the comings and goings of Caracciolo—he openly jested with his wife's follower about his courtship.

"Well, how is it getting on, Luigi?" he asked one day.

"Badly, Cesare. It couldn't be worse," responded Luigi, with a melancholy accent that was only half a feint.

"And yet I left the field free to you."

"Yes; you are as generous as the emperors your namesakes; but when you have captured a province you know how to keep it, whether you are far or near."

"Men of my age always do, Luigi."

"Ah, you have a different tradition."

"What tradition?"

"You don't love."

"What! Do you mean to say that you young fellows love?" asked Cesare, lifting his eyebrows.

"Sometimes, you know, we commit that folly."

"It's a mistaken method—a grave blunder. I hope that you've not fallen into it."

"I don't know," said Luigi, looking mysterious. "Besides, your question strikes me as prompted by jealousy. I'll say no more. It might end in bloodshed."

"I don't think so," laughed Cesare.

"But you'll drive me to despair, Dias. Don't you see that your confidence tortures me. For heaven's sake, do me the favour of being jealous."

"Anything to oblige you, my dear fellow, except that. I've never been jealous of a woman in my life."

"And why not?"

"Because——. One day or another I'll tell you." And putting his arm through Luigi's he led him into the drawing-room of the Hotel Vittoria.

Such talks were frequent between them; on Cesare's side calm and ironical, on Luigi's sometimes a little bitter. On their family outings, Cesare always gave his arm to Laura, for he held it ridiculous for a husband to pair off with his wife; and Caracciolo would devote himself to Anna. Cesare would make him a sign of intelligence, laughing at his assiduity.

"Rigidly obeying orders, eh?" asked the sarcastic husband.

"Anyhow, it's she who's given me my orders," answered the other, sadly.

"But really, Anna, you're putting to death the handsomest lad in Christendom!" exclaimed Cesare.

"The world is the richer for those who die of love," she returned.

"Sentimental aphorism," said Cesare, with a cutting ironical smile.

And he went away to dance with Laura. Between Anna and Luigi there was a long silence. It was impossible for her to listen to these pleasantries without suffering. The idea that her husband could speak thus lightly of another man's love for her, the idea that he could treat as a worldly frivolity the daily siege that Caracciolo was laying to her heart, martyrised her. She was nothing to him, since he could allow another man to court her. He never showed a sign of jealousy, and jealousy pleases women even when they know it is not sincere. She was angry with Cesare as much as with Luigi.

"You jest too much about your feelings for any woman to take them seriously," she said to the latter, one evening, when they were listening to a concert of mandolines and guitars.

"You're right," he answered, turning pale. "But once when I never jested, I had equally bad luck. You refused to marry me."

He spoke sadly. That she had refused to marry him still further embittered for him her present indifference. How could a woman have refused a rich and handsome youth, for a man who had passed forty, and was effete in mind and body? How had Cesare Dias so completely taken possession of this woman's heart? The passion of Anna for Cesare, and that of Caracciolo for Anna, were much talked of in Sorrento society, and the general opinion was that Dias must be a tremendous wizard, that he possessed to a supreme degree the art of attracting men and winning women, and that everybody was right to love and worship him. As for Caracciolo, his was the story of a failure.

Caracciolo himself, moved by I know not what instinct of loyalty, of vanity, or of subtle calculation, accepted and even exaggerated his role of an unsuccessful lover. Wherever he went, at the theatre, at parties, he showed plainly that he was waiting for Anna, and was nervous and restless until she came. His face changed when she entered, bowed to him, gave him her hand; and when she left he followed immediately. Perhaps he was glad that all this should be noticed. He knew he could never move her by appearing cold and sceptical; that was Cesare's pose, and in it Luigi could not hope to rival him. Perhaps her sympathies would be stirred if she saw him ardent and sorrowful.

In the autumn he perceived that Anna was troubled by some new grief. Her joy at the return of Cesare had given place to a strange agitation. She was pale and silent, with dark circles under her eyes. And he realised that whatever faint liking she had had for himself had been blotted out by a sorrow whose causes were unknown to him.

One day he said to her, "Something is troubling you?"

"Yes," she answered frankly.

"Will you tell me what it is?"

"No; I don't wish to," she said, with the same frankness.

"Am I unworthy of your confidence?"

"I can't tell it to you, I can't. It's too horrible," she murmured, with so heart-broken an inflection that he was silent, fearing lest others should witness her emotion.

He returned to the subject later on, but without result. Anna appeared horror-struck by her own thoughts and feelings. Luigi had numberless suspicions. Had Anna secretly come to love him? Or, had she fallen in love with some one else, some one unknown to him? But he soon saw that neither of these suppositions were tenable. He saw that she had not for a moment ceased to love Cesare Dias, and that her grief, whatever it was, sprang as usual from her love for him.

For the first week after his return her husband had been kind and tender to her; then, little by little, he had resumed his old indifference. He constantly neglected her. He went out perpetually with Laura, on the pretext that she was too old now to be accompanied only by her governess, and that it was his duty to find a husband for her. Sometimes Anna went with them, to enjoy her husband's presence.

Often he and Laura would joke together about this question of her marriage.

"How many suitors have you?" asked Cesare, laughing.

"Four who have declared themselves; three or four others who are a little uncertain."

Anna felt herself excluded from their intimacy, and sought in vain to enter it. It made her exceedingly unhappy.

She was jealous of her sister, and she hated herself for her jealousy.

"I am vile and perfidious since I suspect others of vileness and perfidy," she told herself to.

Was it possible that Cesare could be guilty of such a dreadful sin, that he could be making love to Laura?

"What's the matter with you? What are you thinking about?" he asked his wife.

"Nothing, nothing."

"What's the matter?" he insisted.

"Don't ask me, don't ask me," she exclaimed, putting her hand over his mouth.

But one evening, when they were alone, and he again questioned her, she answered, "It's because I love you so, Cesare, I love you so."

"I know it," he said, with a light smile. "But it isn't only that, dear Anna."

And he playfully ruffled up her black hair.

"You're right. It isn't only that. I'm jealous of you, Cesare."

"And of what woman?" he asked, suddenly becoming cold and imperious.

"Of all women. If you so much as touch a woman's hand, I am in despair."

"Of women in general?"

"Of women in general."

"Of no one in particular?"

She hesitated for a moment. "Of no one in particular."

"It's fancy, superstition," he said, pulling his moustache.

"It's love, love," she cried. "Ah, if you should love another, I would kill myself."

"I don't think you'll die a violent death," said he, laughing.

"Remember—darling—I would kill myself."

"You'll live to be eighty, and die in your bed," he said, still laughing.

For a few days she was reassured. But on the first occasion, when her husband and Laura again went out together, her jealousy returned, and she suffered atrociously. Her conduct became odd and extravagant. Sometimes she treated Laura with the greatest kindness; sometimes she was rude to her, and would leave her brusquely, to go and shut herself up in her own room.

Laura asked no questions.

"When are we going to leave Sorrento?" Anna asked. But her husband did not answer, appearing to wish to prolong their sojourn there.

"Let us go away, I beg you, Cesare."

"So soon? Naples is empty at this season. There's nothing to do there. We'd have the air of provincials."

"That doesn't matter. Let us go away, Cesare."

"You are bored, here in the loveliest spot in the world?"

"Sorrento is lovely, but I want to go away."

"As you wish," he said, suddenly consenting. "Give orders to the servants to make ready."

And, to avenge himself, he neglected her utterly during the last two or three days, going off constantly with Laura.

On the eve of their departure Luigi Caracciolo called, to make his adieux. He found Anna alone.

"Good evening, Signora Dias," he said, and the commonplace words had an inflection of melancholy.

"Good evening. You've not gone to the farewell dance at the Vittoria?"

"I have no farewells to give except to you."

"Farewell, then," she said, seating herself near him.

"Farewell," he murmured, smiling, and looking into her eyes. "But we shall meet again within a fortnight."

"I don't know whether I shall be receiving so soon. I don't know whether I shall receive at all."

"You're going to shut your doors to me?" he asked, turning pale.

"Not to you only, to everybody. I'm not made for society. I'm out of place in it, out of tune with it. Solitude suits me better."

"You will die of loneliness. Seeing a few devoted friends will do you good."

"My troubles are too deep."

"Don't you think you're a little selfish? If you shut your doors, others will suffer, and you don't care. You are willing to deprive us of the great pleasure of seeing you. But don't you know that the pain we give reacts upon ourselves? Don't be selfish."

"It's true. I'm perhaps selfish. But who of us is perfect? The most innocent, the purest people in the world, can make others unhappy, without wishing to."

He studied her, feeling that he was near to the secret of her sorrow.

"Sorrento has bored you?" he asked.

"Not exactly bored me. I have been unhappy here."

"More unhappy than at Naples?"

"More than at Naples."

"And why?"

"I don't know. I carry my unhappiness with me."

"Did you imagine that Sorrento would make over the man you love?"

"I hoped——"

"Nothing can make that man over. He's not bad perhaps; but he's what he is."

"It's true."

"Why, then, do you seek the impossible?" he went on.

"And you—aren't you seeking the impossible?" she retorted.

"Yes. But I stop at wishing for it. You see how reasonable I am. You are sad, very sad, Anna, and not for my sake, for another's; yet I should be so happy if I could help you or comfort you in any way."

"Thank you, thank you," she replied, moved.

"I believe that dark days are waiting for you at Naples. I don't wish to prophesy evil, Anna, but that is my belief."

"I'm sure of it," said she, and a sudden desperation showed itself in her face.

"Well, will you treat me as a friend, and remember me in your moments of pain?"

"Yes, I will remember you."

"Will you call me to you?"

"I will call upon you as upon a brother."

"Listen, Anna. Officially I live with my mother in our old family palace. But my real home is the Rey Villa in the Chiatamone. I promise you, Anna, that I am speaking to you now, as I would speak to my dearest sister. Remember this, that, beginning a fortnight hence, I will wait there every day till four o'clock in the afternoon, to hear from you. I shall be quite alone in the house, Anna. You can come without fear, if you need me. Or you can send for me. My dearest hope will be in some way to serve you. I will obey you like a slave. Anna, Anna, when your hour of trouble arrives, remember that I am waiting for you. When you have need of a friend's help, remember that I am waiting."

"But why do you give me your life like this?"

"Because it is good to give it thus. You, if you loved, would you not do the same?"

"I would do the same. I would give my life."

"You see! But forget that word love; it escaped me involuntarily. It is not the man who loves you, it is the devoted friend, it is the brother, whom you are to remember. My every day will be at your disposal. I swear that no unhallowed thought shall move me."

"I believe you," she said.

She gave him her hand. He kissed it.

IV.

Anna was as good as her word, and on her return to Naples shut herself up in solitude and silence, receiving no one, visiting no one, spending much of her time in her own room, going in the morning for long walks in the hope of tiring herself out, speaking but little, and living in a sort of moral somnolence that seemed to dull her sorrows. Her husband and sister continued to enjoy their liberty, as they had enjoyed it at Sorrento. She left them to themselves. She was alternately consumed by suspicions and remorseful for them. In vain she sought comfort from religion, her piety could not bear the contact of her earthly passion, and was destroyed by it. She had gone to her confessor, meaning to tell him everything, but when she found herself kneeling before the iron grating, her courage failed her; she dared not accuse her husband and her sister to a stranger. So she spoke confusedly and vaguely, and the good priest could give her only vague consolation.

She abandoned herself to a complete moral prostration. She passed long hours motionless in her easy-chair, or on her bed, in a sort of stupor and often was absent from table, on one pretext or another.

"The Signora came home an hour ago, and is lying down," said Cesare's man-servant.

"Very good. Don't disturb her," returned his master, with an air of relief.

"The Signora has a headache, and will not come to luncheon," said Anna's maid to Laura.

"Very good. Stay within call, if she should wish for anything," responded Laura, serene and imperturbable.

And Cesare and Laura merrily pursued their intimacy, never bestowing a thought upon her whom they thereby wounded in every fibre of her body, and in the essence of her soul. The anguish of jealousy is like the anguish of death, and Anna suffered it to the ultimate pang, at the same time despising herself for it, telling herself that she was the most unjust of women. Her sister was purity itself; her husband was incapable of evil; they were superior beings, worthy of adoration; and she was daily thinking of them as criminals, and covering them with mire. Often and often, in the rare moments when her husband treated her affectionately, she longed to open her heart and tell him everything. But his manner intimidated her, and she dared not. She wondered whether she might not be mad, and whether her jealousy was not the figment of an infirm mind. She had hoped to find peace in flying from Sorrento; now her hope was undeceived; and Anna understood that her pain came from within, not from without. To see her sister and her husband together, seated side by side, walking arm in arm, pressing each other's hands, looking and smiling at each other, was more than she could bear; she fled their presence; she left the house for long wanderings in the streets, or shut herself up in her own room, knowing but too well that they would not notice her absence. Indeed, it would be like a burden taken from their shoulders, for she was a burden to them, with her pallor and her speechlessness.

"They are gay, and I bore them," she told herself.

On several occasions, Cesare twitted her on the subject of her continual melancholy, demanding its cause; but Anna, smarting under his sarcasms, could not answer him. One day, in great irritation, he declared that she had no right to go about posing as a victim, for she wasn't a victim, and her sentimental vapourings bored him immensely.

"Ah, I bore you; I bore you," cried Anna, shaking with suppressed sobs.

"Yes, unspeakably. And I hope that some day or another you'll stop boring me, do you hear?"

"I had better die. That would be best," she sighed.

"But can't you live and be less tiresome? Is it a task, a mission, that you have undertaken, to bore people?"

"I had better die, better die," she sobbed.

He went off abruptly, cursing his lot, cursing above all the monstrous error he had made in marrying this foolish creature. And she, who had wished to ask his pardon, found herself alone. Later in the same day she noticed that Laura treated her with a certain contempt, shrugging her shoulders at the sight of her eyes red from weeping.

Anna determined that she would try to take on at least the external appearances of contentment. The beautiful Neapolitan winter was beginning. She had eight or ten new frocks made, and resolved to become frivolous and vain. Whenever she went out she invariably met Luigi Caracciolo; it was as if she had forewarned him of her itinerary. He had divined it, with that fine intuition which lovers have. They never stopped to speak, however; they simply bowed and passed on. But in his way of looking at her she could read the words of their understanding—"Remember, every day, till four o'clock."

She threw herself into the excitements of society, going much to the theatre and paying many calls. Cesare encouraged this new departure.

The people amongst whom she moved agreed that she was very attractive, but whispered that one day or another she would do something wild.

"What?"

"Oh, something altogether extravagant."

One evening towards the end of January Anna was going to the San Carlo; it was a first night. At dinner she asked Laura if she would care to accompany her.

"No," answered Laura, absently.

"Why not?"

"I've got to get up early to-morrow morning, to go to Confession."

"Ah, very well. And you—will you come, Cesare?"

"Yes," he said, hesitating a little.

"Cousin Scibilia is coming too," Anna added.

"Then, if you will permit me, I'll not come till the second act." And he smiled amiably.

"Have you something to do?"

"Yes; but we'll come home together."

Anna turned red and white. There was something half apologetic in her husband's tone, as if he had a guilty conscience in regard to her. But what did that matter? The prospect of coming home together, alone in a closed carriage, delighted her.

She went to dress for the theatre. She put on for the first time a gown of blue brocade, with a long train, bold in colour, but admirably setting off the rich ivory of Anna's complexion. In her black hair she fixed three diamond stars. She wore no bracelets, but round her throat a single string of pearls. When she was dressed, she sent for her husband.

"You're looking most beautiful," he said.

He took her hands and kissed them; then he kissed her fair round arms; and then he kissed her lips. She thrilled with joy and bowed her head.

"We'll meet at the theatre," he said, "and come home together."

She called for the Marchesa Scibilia, who now lived in the girls' old house in the Via Gerolomini. And they drove on towards the theatre. But when they reached the Toledo they were met by a number of carriages returning. The explanation of this the two ladies learned under the portico of the San Carlo. Over the white play-bill a notice was posted announcing the sudden indisposition of the prima-donna, and informing the public that there would accordingly be no performance that evening. Anna had a lively movement of disappointment, jumping out of her *coupé* to read the notice for herself.

Luigi Caracciolo was waiting in the shadow of a pillar, sure that she would come.

"Marchesa, you have a very ferocious cousin," he said, stepping forward to kiss the old lady's hand, and laughing at Anna's manifest anger. Then he bowed to her, and in his eyes there was the eternal message, "Remember, I wait for you every day."

She shook her head in the darkness. She was bitterly disappointed. Her evening was lost—the evening during which she had counted upon being alone with Cesare in their box, alone with him in the carriage, alone with him at home. And her beautiful blue gown; she had put it on to no purpose.

"What shall we do?" she asked her cousin.

"I'm going home. I don't care to go anywhere else. And you?"

"I'm going home, too."

She half hoped that she might still find Cesare at the house, and so have at least a half hour with him before he went out. He was very slow about dressing; he never hurried, even when he had an urgent appointment. Perhaps she would find him in his room, tying his white tie, putting a flower in his button-hole. She deposited the Marchesa Scibilia at the palace in the Via Gerolomini, and bade her coachman hurry home.

"Has the Signore gone out?" she asked the porter.

No, he had not gone out. The porter was about to pull his bell-cord, to ring for a footman, but Anna instinctively stopped him. She wished to surprise her husband. She put her finger to her lips, smiling, as she met one of the maids, and crossed the house noiselessly, arriving thus at the door of Cesare's room, the door that gave upon the vestibule, not the one which communicated with the passage between his room and Anna's.

The door was not locked. She opened it softly. She would surprise her husband so merrily. But, having opened the door, she found herself still in darkness, for Cesare had lowered the two *portières* of heavy olive velvet.

A sudden interior force prevented Anna's lifting the curtains and showing herself. She remained there behind them, perfectly concealed, and able to see and hear everything that went on in the room, through an aperture.

Cesare was in his dress-suit, with an immaculate white waistcoat, a watch-chain that went from his waistcoat-pocket to the pocket of his trousers, with a beautiful white gardenia in his button-hole, his handsome black moustaches freshly curled, and his whole air one of profound satisfaction. He was seated in a big leather arm-chair, his fine head resting on its brown cushions, against which the pallor of his face stood out charmingly.

He was not alone.

Laura, dressed in that soft white wool which seemed especially woven for her supple and flowing figure, with a bouquet of white roses in the cincture that passed twice loosely round her waist, with her blonde hair artistically held in place by small combs of tortoise-shell, and forming a sort of aureole about her brow and temples, the glory of her womanly beauty—Laura was in Cesare's room.

She was not seated on one of his olive velvet sofas, nor on one of his stools of carved wood, nor in one of his leather easy-chairs. She was seated on the arm of the chair in which he himself reclined; she was seated side wise, swinging one of her little feet, in a black slipper richly embroidered with pearls, and an open-work black silk stocking.

One of her arms was extended across the cushion above Cesare's head; and, being higher up than he, she had to bend down, to speak into his face. She was smiling, a strange, deep smile, such as had never been seen before upon the pure red curve of her lips.

Cesare, with his face turned up, was looking at her; and every now and then he took her hand and kissed it, a kiss that lingered, lingered while she changed colour.

He kissed her hand, and she was silent, and he was silent; but it was not a sad silence, not a thoughtful silence. It was a silence in which they seemed to find an unutterable pleasure. They found an unutterable pleasure in their silence, their solitude, their freedom, their intimate companionship, in the kiss he had just given her, and which was the forerunner of many others.

Anna had arrived behind the curtain at the very moment when Cesare was kissing Laura's hand. She saw them gazing into each other's eyes, speechless with their emotion. Anna could hear nothing but the tumultuous beating of her own heart, a beating that leapt up to her throat, making it too throb tumultuously.

The fine white hand of Laura remained in Cesare's, softly surrendered to him; then, as if the mere contact were not enough, his and her fingers closely interlaced themselves. The girl, who had not removed her eyes from his, smiled languorously, as if all her soul were in her hand, joined now for ever to the hand of Cesare; a smile that confessed herself conquered, yet proclaimed herself triumphant.

They did not speak. But their story spoke for itself.

Anna saw how close they were to each other, saw how their hands were joined, saw the glances of passionate tenderness that they exchanged. Clearly, in every detail, she witnessed this silent scene of love. Her heart, her temples, her pulses, pounded frightfully; her nerves palpitated; and she said to herself:

"Oh, I am dreaming, I am dreaming."

Like one dreaming, indeed, she was unable to move, unable to cry out; her tongue clove to the roof of her mouth; she could not lift the curtains; she could not advance, she could not tear herself away. She could only stand there rigid as stone, and behold the dreadful vision. Every line of it, every passing expression on Cesare's or Laura's face, burned itself into her brain with fierce and terrible precision. And in her tortured heart she was conscious of but one mute, continuous, childlike prayer—not to see any longer that which she saw—to be freed from her nightmare, waked from her dream. And all her inner forces were bent upon the effort to close her eyes, to lower her eyelids, and put a veil between her and that sight. Her prayer was not answered; she could not close her eyes.

Laura took her bouquet of white roses from her belt, and playfully struck Cesare's shoulder with them. Then she raised them to her face, breathing in their perfume, and kissing them. Smiling, she offered Cesare the roses that she had kissed, and he with his lips drank her kisses from them. After that, she kissed them again, convulsively, turning away her head. Their eyes burned, his and hers. Again he sought her kisses amongst the roses; and she put down her face to kiss them anew, at the same time with him. And slowly, from the cold, fragrant roses, their lips turned, and met in a kiss. Their hands were joined, their faces were near together, their lips met in a kiss, and their eyes that had burned, softened with fond light.

"Perhaps I am mad," Anna said to herself, hearing the wild blows of the blood in her brain.

And, to make sure, wishing to be convinced that it was all an hallucination, she prayed that they might speak; perhaps they were mere phantoms sent to kill her. No sound issued from their lips.

"Lord, Lord—a word," she prayed in her heart. "A sound—a proof that they are real, or that they are spectres."

She heard, indeed, a deep sigh. It came from Laura, after their long kiss. The girl jumped up, freed her hands from Cesare's, and took two or three steps into the room. She was nearer to Anna now. Her cheeks were red, her hair was ruffled; and she, with a vague, unconscious movement, lifted it up behind her ears. Her lips were parted in a smile that revealed her dazzling teeth. Her gaze wandered, proud and sad.

"Heaven, heaven give her strength to go away. Give her strength, give me strength," prayed Anna, in her dream, in her madness.

But Laura had not the strength to go away. She returned to Cesare; she sat down at his feet, looking up at him, smiling upon him, holding his hand, adoring him. And Cesare, his eyes filled with tears, kissed her lips again and again—a torrent of kisses.

"Cesare cannot weep. They are phantoms. I am mad," said Anna. A terrible fire leapt from her heart to her brain, making her tremble as in a fever; and then a sudden cold seemed to freeze her. She had heard. These phantoms had spoken. They were a man and a woman; they were her husband, Cesare, and her sister Laura. Laura had drawn away from Cesare's fury of kisses, and was standing beside him, while he, still seated, held her two hands. They were smiling upon each other.

"Do you love me?" he asked.

"I love you," answered Laura.

"How much do you love me?"

"So much! So much!"

"But how much?"

"Absolutely."

"And—how long will you love me, Laura?"

"Always."

Now Anna was shivering with cold. She was not mad. She was not dreaming. Her teeth chattered. It seemed as if she had been standing there for a century. She dreaded being discovered, as if she were guilty of a crime. But she could not move, she could not go away. It was too much, too much; she could not endure it! She covered her mouth with her fan, to suffocate her voice, to keep from crying out, and cursing God and love. Laura began to speak.

"Do you love me?" she asked.

"Yes, I love you."

"How much do you love me?"

"With all my heart, Laura."

"How long have you loved me?"

"Always."

"How long will you love me?"

"Always."

Unendurable, unendurable! A wild anger tempted Anna to enter the room, to tear down the curtains, to scream. It was unendurable.

Cesare said to Laura, very softly, "Go away now."

"Why, love?"

"Go away. It is late. You must go."

"Ah, you're a bad love—bad!"

"Don't say that. Don't look like that. Go away, Laura."

And fondly, he put his arm round her waist and led her to the door.

She moved reluctantly, leaning her head upon his shoulder, looking up at him tenderly.

At the door they kissed again.

"Good-bye, love," said Laura.

"Good-bye, love," said Cesare.

The girl went away.

Cesare came back, looking exhausted, deathlike. He lit a cigarette.

Anna, holding her breath, crossed the vestibule, the smoking-room, the drawing-room, and at last reached her own room, and shut her door behind her. She had run swiftly, instinctively, with the instinct that guides a wounded animal. Her maid came and knocked. She called to her that she did not need her. Then some one else knocked.

"Anna, Anna," said the calm voice of her husband.

"What do you want?" She had to lean on a chair, to keep from falling; her voice was dull.

"Was there no performance? Or were you ill?"

"There was no performance."

"Have you just returned?"

"Yes, just returned." But the lie made her blush.

"And your Highness is invisible? I should like to pay your Highness my respects."

"No," she answered, with a choking voice.

"Good-bye, love," he called.

"Oh, infamous, infamous!" she cried.

But he had already moved away, and did not hear.

For a long while she lay on her bed, burying her face in her pillow, biting it, to keep down her sobs. She was shivering with cold, in spite of the feather coverlet she had drawn over her. All her flesh and spirit were in furious revolt against the thing that she had seen and heard.

She rose, and looked round her room. It was in disorder—the dress she had worn, her fan, her jewels tossed pell-mell hither and thither. Slowly, with minute care, she gathered these objects up, and put them in their places.

Then she rang the bell.

Her maid came, half asleep.

"What time is it?" asked Anna, forgetting that on the table beside her stood the clock that Cesare had given her.

"It's one," responded the maid.

"So late?" inquired her mistress. "You may go to bed."

"And your Excellency?"

"You can do nothing for me."

But the maid began to smooth down the bed. Feeling the pillow wet with tears, she said, with the affectionate familiarity of Neapolitan servants, "Whoever is good suffers."

The words went through her heart like a knife. Perhaps the servant knew. Perhaps she, Anna, had been the only blind member of the household. The whole miserable story of her desertion and betrayal was known and commented upon by her servants; and she was an object of their pity! Whoever is good suffers!

"Good night, your Excellency, and may you sleep well," said the maid.

"Thank you. Good-night."

She was alone again. She had not had the courage to ask whether her husband had come home; he was most probably out, amusing himself in society.

For a half hour she lay on her sofa; then she got up. A big lamp burned on her table, but before going away her maid had lighted another lamp, a little ancient Pompeian lamp of bronze that in old times had doubtless lighted Pompeian ladies to their trysts.

Anna took this lamp and left her room. The house was dark and silent. She moved towards Laura's room; and suddenly she remembered another night, like this, when she had stolen through a dark sleeping house to join Giustino Morelli on the terrace, and offer to fly with him. Giustino Morelli, who was he? what was he? A shadow, a dream. A thing that had passed utterly from her life.

At her sister's door she paused for a moment, then she opened it noiselessly, and guided by the light of her lamp, approached her sister's bed. Laura was sleeping peacefully; Anna held up her lamp and looked at her.

She smiled in her sleep.

"Laura!" Anna called, so close to her that her breath fell on her cheek. "Laura!"

Her sister moved slightly, but did not wake.

"Laura! Laura!"

Her sister sat up. She appeared frightened for a moment, but then she composed herself with an effort.

"It is I, Laura," said Anna, putting her lamp on a table.

"I see you," returned Laura.

"Get up and come with me."

"What for?"

"Get up and come, Laura."

"Where, Anna?"

"Get up and come," said Anna, implacably.

"I won't obey you."

"Oh, you'll come," cried Anna, with an imperious smile.

"You're mistaken. I'll not come."

"You'll come, Laura."

"No, Anna."

"You're very much afraid of me then?"

"Here I am. I'll go where you like," Laura said, proudly, resenting the imputation of fear. And she began to dress.

Anna waited for her, standing up. Laura proceeded calmly with her toilet. But when she came to put on her frock of white wool, Anna had a mad access of rage, and covered her face with her hands, to shut out the sight. Four hours ago, only four hours ago, in that same frock, Laura had been kissed by Cesare. Her sister seemed to her the living image of treachery.

Laura moved about the room as if she was hunting for something.

"What are you doing?" asked Anna.

"I am looking for something."

And she drew from under a pocket-handkerchief her bunch of white roses.

"Throw those flowers away," cried Anna.

"And why?"

"Throw those flowers away, Laura, Laura."

"No."

"By our Lady of Sorrows, I beseech you, throw them away."

"You have threatened me. You have no further right to beseech me," said Laura quietly, putting the flowers in her belt.

"Oh God!" cried Anna, pressing her hands to her temples.

"Let us go," she said at last.

Laura followed her across the silent house to her room.

"Sit down," said Anna.

"I am waiting," said Laura.

"Then you don't understand?" asked Anna, smiling.

"No—I understand nothing."

"Can't you imagine?"

"I have no imagination."

"And your heart—does your heart tell you nothing, Laura? Laura, Laura, does your conscience tell you nothing?"

"Nothing," said the other quietly, lifting up the rich blonde hair behind her ears. The same gesture that Anna had seen her make in Cesare's room.

"Laura, you are my husband's mistress," Anna said, raising her arms towards heaven.

"You're mad, Anna."

"My husband's mistress, Laura."

"You're mad."

"Oh, liar, liar! Disloyal and vile woman, who has not even the courage of her love!" cried Anna, starting up, with flaming eyes.

"Beware, Anna, beware. Strong language at a moment like this is dangerous. Say what you've got to say clearly; but don't insult me. Don't insult me, because your diseased imagination happens to be excited. Do you understand?"

"Oh, heavens, heavens!" exclaimed Anna.

"But you can see for yourself, you're mad. You see, you have nothing to say to justify your insults."

"Oh, Madonna, Madonna, give me strength," prayed Anna, wringing her hands.

"Do you see?" asked Laura. "You've called me here to vilify my innocence."

"Laura," said poor Anna, trembling, "Laura, it's no guess of mine, no inference, that you are my husband's mistress. I have not read it in any anonymous letter. No servant has told me it. In such a case as this no one has a right to believe an anonymous letter or a servant's denunciation. One cannot on such grounds withdraw one's respect from a person whom one loves."

"Well, Anna."

"But I have seen, I have seen," she cried, prey to so violent an emotion that it seemed to her as if the thing she had seen was visible before her again.

"What have you seen?" asked Laura, suddenly.

"Oh, horrible, horrible," cried Anna, remembering her vision.

"What have you seen?" repeated Laura, seizing Anna's arm.

"Oh, what a dreadful thing, what a dreadful thing," she sobbed, covering her face with her hands.

But Laura was herself consumed with anger and pain; and she drew Anna's hands from her face, and insisted, "Now—at this very moment—you have got to tell me what you have seen. Do you understand?"

And the other, turning pale at her threatening tone, replied: "You wish to know what I have seen, Laura? And you ask me in a rage of offended innocence, of wounded virtue? You are angry, Laura? Angry—you? What right have you to be angry, or to speak to me as you have done? Aren't you afraid? Have you no fear, no suspicions, nothing? You threaten me; you tell me I am mad. You want to know what I have seen; and you are haughty because you deem yourself secure, and me a madwoman. But, to be secure, you should close the doors behind you when you go to an assignation. When you are speaking of love, and kissing, to be secure you should close the doors, Laura, close the doors."

"I don't understand you," murmured Laura, very pale.

"This evening, at nine o'clock, when you were in Cesare's room—I came home suddenly—you weren't expecting me—you were alone, secure—and I saw through the door——"

"What?" demanded the other, with bowed head.

"As much as can be seen and heard. Remember."

Laura fell into a chair.

"Why have you done this? Why? Why?" asked Anna.

Laura did not answer.

"Don't you dare to answer? Oh, see how base you are! See how perfidious you are. What manner of woman are you? Why did you do it?"

"Because I love Cesare."

"O Lord, Lord!" cried Anna, breaking into desperate sobs.

"Don't you know it? Haven't your eyes seen it? haven't your ears heard it? Do you imagine that a woman such as I am goes into a man's room if she doesn't love him! That she lets him kiss her, that she kisses him, unless she loves him! What more have you to ask! I love Cesare."

"Be quiet, be quiet, be quiet," said Anna.

"And Cesare loves me," Laura went on.

"Be quiet. You are my sister. You are a young girl. Don't speak such an infamy. Be quiet. Don't say that you and Cesare are two monsters."

"You have seen us together. I love Cesare, and he loves me."

"Monstrous, infamous!"

"It may be infamous, but it is so."

"But don't you realise what you are doing! Don't you feel that it is infamous; Don't you understand how dreadful your offence is! Am I not your sister—I whom you are betraying!"

"I loved Cesare from the beginning. You betrayed me."

"The excuse of guilt! I loved him, I love him. You are betraying me."

"You love him stupidly, and bore him; I love him well."

"He's a married man."

"He was married by force, Anna."

"He is my husband."

"Oh, very slightly!"

"Laura!" exclaimed Anna, wounded to the quick, she who was all wounds.

"I'm not blind," said Laura, tranquilly. "I can take in the situation."

"But your conscience! But your religion! But your modesty, which is soiled by such an atrocious sin!"

"I'm not your husband's mistress, you know that yourself."

"But you love him. You thrill at the touch of his hand. You kiss him. You tell him you love him."

"Well, all that doesn't signify that I'm his mistress."

"The sin is as great."

"No, it's not as great, Anna."

"It's a deadly sin merely to love another woman's husband."

"But I'm not his mistress. Be exact."

"A change of words; the sin is the same."

"Words have their importance; they are the symbols of facts."

"It's an infamy," said Anna.

"Anna, don't insult me."

"Insult you! Do you pretend that that pretty pure face of yours is capable of blushing under an insult? Can your chaste brow be troubled by an insult? You have trampled all innocence and all modesty under foot—you, the daughter of my mother! You have broken your sister's heart—you, the daughter of the same mother! And now you say that I insult you. Good!"

"You have no right to insult me."

"I haven't the right? Before such treachery? I haven't the right? Before such dishonour?"

"If you will call upon your memory, you will see that you haven't the right."

"What do you wish me to remember?"

"A single circumstance. Once upon a time, you, a girl like me, abandoned your home, and eloped with a man you loved, a nobody, a poor obscure nobody. Then you deceived me, Cesare, and everybody else. By that elopement you dishonoured the graves of your father and mother, and you dishonoured your name which is also mine."

"Oh, heavens, heavens, heavens!" cried Anna.

"You passed a whole day out of Naples, in an inn at Pompeii, alone the whole day with a man you loved, in a private room."

"I wasn't Giustino Morelli's mistress."

"Exactly. Nor am I Cesare Dias'."

"I wasn't Giustino Morelli's mistress," repeated Anna.

"I wasn't behind the door, as you were, to see the truth."

"Oh, cruel, wicked sister—cruel and wicked!"

"And please to have the fairness to remember that on that day Cesare Dias rushed to your rescue. In charity, without saying a word to reproach you, he brought you back to the home you had deserted. In charity, without insulting you, I opened my arms to welcome you. In charity we nursed you through your long illness, and never once did we reproach you. You see, you see, you're unjust and ungrateful."

"But you have wounded me in my love, Laura. But I adore Cesare, and I am horribly jealous of him. I can't banish the thought of your love for him; I can remember nothing but your kisses. I feel as if I were going mad. Oh, Laura, Laura, you who were so pure and beautiful, you who are worthy of a young man's love, why do you throw away your life and your honour for Cesare?"

"But you? Don't you also love him? You too are young. Yet didn't you love him so desperately that you would gladly have died, if he hadn't married you? I have followed your example, that is all. As you love him, I love him, Anna. We are sisters, and the same passion burns in our veins."

"Don't say that, don't say it. My love will last as long as my life, Laura."

"And so will mine."

"Don't say it, don't say it."

"Until I die, Anna."

"Don't say it."

"My blood is like yours; my nerves are like yours; my heart is as ardent as yours. My soul is consumed with love, as yours is. We are the daughters of the same parents. Cesare has fascinated you, Cesare has fascinated me."

"Oh, heavens, heavens! I must kill myself then. I must die!"

"Bah!" said Laura, with a movement of disdain.

"I will kill myself, Laura."

"Those who say it don't do it."

"You are deceiving yourself, wicked, scornful creature."

"Those who say it don't do it," repeated Laura, laughing bitterly.

"But understand me! I can't endure this betrayal. Understand! I—I alone have the right to love Cesare. He is mine. I won't give him up to anybody. My only refuge, my only comfort, my only consolation is in my love. Don't you see that I have nothing else?"

"Luigi Caracciolo loves you, though," said Laura, smiling.

"What are you saying to me?"

"You might fall in love with him."

"You propose an infamy to me."

"But consider. I love Cesare; Cesare loves me and not you. But Caracciolo loves you. Well, why not fall in love with him?"

"Because it would be infamous."

"You are beginning to insult me again, Anna. It is late. I am going away."

"No, don't go yet, Laura. Think how terrible this thing is for me. Listen to me, Laura, and call to aid all your kindness. I have insulted you, it is true; but you can't know what jealousy is like, you can't imagine the unendurable torture of it. Call to aid your goodness, Laura. Think—we were nourished at the same breast, the same mother's hands caressed us. Think—we have made our journey in life together. Laura, Laura, my sister! You have betrayed me; you have outraged me; in the past seven hours I have suffered all that it is humanly possible to suffer; you can't know what jealousy is like. Don't be impatient. Listen to me. It is a terrible moment. Don't laugh. I am not exaggerating. Listen to me carefully. Laura, all that you have done, I forget it, I forgive it. Do you hear? I forgive you. I am sure your heart is good. You will understand all the affection and all the meekness there are in my forgiveness."

And as if it were she who were the guilty one, she knelt before her sister, taking her hand, kissing it, bathing it with her tears. Laura, seeing this woman whom she had so cruelly wronged kneel before her, closed her eyes, and for a moment was intensely pale. But her soul was strong; she was able to conquer her emotion. For an instant she was silent; then, coming to the supreme question of their existence, she demanded: "And what do you expect in exchange for this pardon?" She had the air of according a favour.

"Laura, Laura, you must be good and great, since I have forgiven you."

"What is your price for this forgiveness?"

"You must not love Cesare any more. Bravely you must cast that impure love out of your soul, which it degrades. You must not love him any more. And then, not only will my pardon be complete and absolute, but you will find in me the fondest and tenderest of sisters. I will devote my life to proving to you how much I love you. My sole desire will be to make you happy; I will be your best and surest friend. But you must be good and strong, Laura; you must remember that you are my sister; you must forget Cesare."

"Anna, I cannot."

"Listen, listen. Don't answer yet. Don't decide yet. Don't speak the last word yet, the awful word. Think, Laura, it is your future, it is your life, that you are staking upon this love: a black future, a fatal certainty of death, if you persist in it. But, on the contrary, if you forget it—if a chaste and innocent impulse of affection for me persuades you to put it from you—what peace, what calm! You will find another man, a worthier man, a man of your own loftiness of spirit, who will understand you, who will make you happy, whom you can love with all your soul, in the consciousness of having done your duty. You will be a happy wife, your husband will be a happy man, you will be a mother, you will have children—you will have children, you! But you must not love Cesare any more."

"Anna, I can't help it."

"Laura, don't make your mind up yet. For pity's sake, hear me. We must find a way out of it, an escape. You will travel, you will make a journey, a long journey, abroad; that will interest you. I'll ask Cousin Scibilia to go with you. She has nothing to detain her; she's a widow; she will go. You will travel. You can't think how travelling relieves one's sufferings. You will see new countries, beautiful countries, where your mind will rise high above the petty, every-day miseries of life. Laura, Laura, see how I pray you, see how I implore you. We have the same blood in our veins. We are children of the same mother. You must not love Cesare any more."

"Anna, I can't help it."

Anna moved towards her sister; but when she found herself face to face with her, an impulse of horror repelled her. She went to the window and stood there, gazing out into the street, into the great shadow of the night. When she came back, her face was cold, austere, self-contained. Her sister felt that she could read a menace in it.

"Is that your last word?" asked Anna.

"My last word."

"You don't think you can change?"

"I don't think so."

"You know what you are doing?"

"Yes, I know."

"And you face the danger?"

"Where is the danger?" asked Laura, rising.

"Don't be afraid, don't be afraid," said Anna, carrying her pocket-handkerchief to her lips and biting it. "I ask you if it doesn't strike you as dangerous that two women such as I, Anna Dias, and you, Laura Acquaviva, should live together in the same house and love the same man with the same passion?"

"It is certainly very dangerous," said Laura slowly, standing up, and looking into her sister's eyes.

"Leave me my husband, Laura," cried Anna, impetuously.

"Take him back—if you can. But you can't, you know. You never could."

"You're a monster. Go away," cried Anna, clenching her teeth, clenching her fists, driving her nails into her flesh.

"It's at your bidding that I'm here. I came to show that I wasn't afraid of you, that's all."

"Go away, monster, monster, monster!"

"Kill me, if you like; but don't call me by that name," cried Laura, at last exasperated.

"You deserve that I should kill you, it is true. By all the souls that hear me, by the souls of our dead parents, by the Madonna, who, with them, is shuddering in heaven at your crime, you deserve that I should kill you!"

"But Cesare would weep for me," taunted Laura, again mistress of herself.

"It is true," rejoined Anna, icily. "Go away then. Go at once."

"Good-bye, Anna."

"Good-bye, Laura."

Leisurely, collectedly, she turned her back upon her sister, and moved away, erect and supple in her white frock, with her light regular footstep. Her hand turned the knob of the door, but on the threshold she paused, involuntarily, and looked at Anna, who stood in the middle of the room with her head bowed, her cheeks colourless, her eyes expressionless, her lips violet and slightly parted, testifying to her fatigue. Laura's hesitation was but momentary. Shrugging her shoulders at that spectacle of sorrow, she closed the door behind her, and went off through the darkness to her own room.

Anna was alone. And within herself she was offering up thanks to the Madonna for having that night saved her from a terrible temptation. For, from the dreadful scene that had just passed, only one thought remained to her. She had besought her sister not to love Cesare any more, promising in exchange all the devotion of her soul and body; and Laura had thrice responded, obstinately, blindly, "I can't help it." Well, when for the third time she heard those words, a sudden, immense fury of jealousy had seized her; suddenly a great red cloud seemed to fall before her eyes, and the redness came from a wound in her sister's white throat, a wound which she had inflicted; and the pale girl lay at her feet lifeless, unable for ever to say again that she loved Cesare and would not cease to love him. Ah, for a minute, for a minute, murder had breathed in Anna's poor distracted heart, and she had wished to kill the daughter of her mother! Now, with spent eyes, feeling herself lost and dying at the bottom of an abyss, she uttered a deep prayer of thanksgiving to God, for that He had swept the red cloud away, for that He had allowed her to suffer without avenging herself. Slowly, slowly she sank upon her knees, she clasped her hands, she said over all the old simple prayers of her childhood, the holy prayers of innocence, praying that still, through all the hopeless misery that awaited her, she might ever be what she had been to-night, a woman capable of suffering everything, incapable of revenge. And in this pious longing her soul seemed to be lifted up, far above all earthly pain.

All her womanly goodness and weakness were mingled in her renunciation of revenge.

The violent energy which she had shown in her talk with Laura had given place to a mortal lassitude. She remained on her knees, and continued to murmur the words of her orisons, but now she no longer understood their meaning. Her head was whirling, as in the beginning of a swoon. She dragged herself with difficulty to her bed, and threw herself upon it, inert as a dead body, in utter physical exhaustion.

Laura had undone her. The whole long scene between them repeated itself over and over in her mind; again she passed from tears to anger, from jealousy to pleading affection; again she saw her sister's pure white face, and the cynical smile that disfigured it, and its hard incapacity for pity, fear, or contrition. Laura had overthrown her, conquered her, undone her. Anna had gone to her, strong in her outraged rights, strong in her offended love, strong in her knowledge of her sister's treachery; she had expected to see that proud brow bend before her, red with shame; she had expected to see those fair hands clasped and trembling, imploring pardon; she had expected to hear that clear voice utter words of penitence and promises of atonement. But far from that, far from accepting the punishment she had earned, the guilty woman had boldly defended her guilt; she had refused with fierce courage to give way; she had clung to her infamy, challenging her sister to do her worst. Anna understood that not one word that she had spoken had made the least impression upon Laura's heart, had stirred in it the faintest movement of generosity or affection; she understood that from beginning to end she had failed and blundered, knowing neither how to punish nor how to forgive.

"I did not kill her. She has beaten me!" she thought.

And yet Anna was in the right; and Laura, by all human and all moral law, was in the wrong. To love a married man, to love her sister's husband, almost her own brother! Anna was right before God, before mankind, before Cesare and Laura themselves. If, when her sister had refused to surrender her husband to her, she had killed her, no human being would have blamed her for it.

"And yet I did not kill her. She has beaten me!"

She tried to find the cause of her defeat, overwhelmed by the despair with which good people see wrong and injustice triumph. She sought for the cause of her defeat, but she could find none, none. She was right—according to all laws, human and divine, she was in the right; she alone was right. Oh, her agony was insupportable, more and more dreadful as she got farther from the fact, and could see it in its full hideousness, examine and analyse it in its full infamy.

"Beaten, beaten, beaten! bitterly worsted and overwhelmed!"

For the third time in her life she had been utterly defeated. She had not known how to defend herself; she had not known how to assert her rights, and conquer. On that fatal day at Pompeii, when Giustino Morelli had abandoned her; on that fatal night at Sorrento, when Cesare Dias had proposed his mephistophelian bargain to her, whereby she was to renounce love, dignity, and her every prerogative as a woman and a wife; at Pompeii and at Sorrento she had been worsted by those who were in the wrong, by Giustino Morelli who could not love, by Cesare Dias who would not.

And now again to-night—to-night, for the third time—betrayed by her husband and her sister—she had not known how to conquer. At Naples, as at Pompeii, as at Sorrento, she who was in the right had been defeated by one who was in the wrong.

"But why? why?" she asked herself, in despair.

She did not know. It was contrary to all reason and all justice. She could only see the fact, clear, cruel, inexorable.

It was destiny. A secret power fought against her, and baffled every effort she attempted. It was a fatality which she bore within herself, a fatality which it was useless to resist. All she could wish for now was that the last word might be spoken soon.

"I must seek the last word," she thought.

She rose from her bed, and looked at the clock. It was four in the morning.

She went to her writing-desk, and, leaning her head upon her hand, tried to think what she had come there to do. Then she took a sheet of paper, and wrote a few words upon it. But when she read them over, they displeased her; she tore the paper up, and threw it away. She wrote and tore up three more notes; at last she was contented with this one:

"Cesare, I must say something to you at once. As soon as you read these words, no matter at what hour of the night or morning, come to my room.—ANNA."

She sealed the note in an envelope, and addressed it to her husband. She left her room, to go to his. The door was locked; she could see no light, hear no sound within. She slipped the letter through the crack above the threshold.

"Cesare shall speak the last word," she thought.

She returned to her own room, and threw herself upon her bed to watch and wait for him.

V.

Anna got up and opened her window, to let in the sun, but it was a grey morning, grey in sky and sea. Lead-coloured clouds rested on the hill of Posillipo; and the wide Neapolitan landscape looked as if it had been covered with ashes. Few people were in the streets; and the palm in the middle of the Piazza Vittoria waved its long branches languidly in the wintry breeze.

Her eyes were burning and her eyelids were heavy. She went into her dressing-room and bathed her face in cold water. Then she combed her hair and fastened it up with a big gold pin. And then she put on a gown of black wool, richly trimmed with jet, a morning street costume. Was she going out? She did not know. She dressed herself in obedience to the necessity which women feel at certain hours of the day to occupy themselves with their toilets. But when she came to fasten her brooch, a clover leaf set with black pearls, that Laura had given her for a wedding-present, she discovered that one of the pearls was gone. The clover-leaf brings luck, but now this one was broken, and its power was gone.

Eleven o'clock struck, and somebody tapped discreetly at the door. She could not find her voice, to answer.

The knock was repeated.

"Come in," she said feebly.

Cesare entered, calm and composed, carrying his hat and ebony walking-stick in his hand.

"Good-morning. Are you going out?" he asked tranquilly.

"No. I don't know," she answered, with a vague gesture.

All her nerves were tingling, as she looked at the traitor's handsome, wasted face, a face so quiet and smiling.

"You had something to say to me?" he reminded her, wrinkling his brow a little.

"Yes."

"I came home late. I didn't want to disturb you," he said, producing a cigarette, and asking permission with a glance to light it.

"You would not have disturbed me."

"I suppose it's nothing of much importance."

"It's a thing of great importance, Cesare."

"As usual," he said, with the shadow of a smile.

"I swear to you by the memory of my mother that nothing is more important."

"Goodness gracious! Act three, scene four!" he exclaimed ironically.

"Scene last," she said, dully, tearing a few beads from her dress, and fingering them.

"So much the better, if we are near the end. The play was rather long, my dear." He was tapping his boot with his walking-stick.

"We will cut it short, Cesare. I have a favour to ask of you. Will you grant it?"

"Ask, oh lovely lady; and in spite of the fact that last night you closed your door upon me, here I am, ready to serve you."

"I have a favour to ask, Cesare."

"Ask it, then, before I go out."

"I want to make a long journey with you—to be gone a year."

"A second honeymoon? The like was never known."

"A journey of a year, do you understand? Take me as your travelling companion, your friend, your servant. For a year, away from here, far away."

"Taking with us our sister, our governess, our dog, our cat, and the whole menagerie?"

"We two alone," she said.

"Ah," said he.

"What is your decision?"

"I will think about it."

"No. You must decide at once."

"What's the hurry? Are we threatened with an epidemic?"

"Decide now."

"Then I decide—no," he said.

"And why?" she asked, turning pale.

"Because I won't."

"Tell me your reason."

"I don't wish to travel."

"You have always enjoyed travelling."

"Well, I enjoy it no more. I am tired, I am old, I will stay at home."

"I implore you, let us go away, far from here."

"But why do you want to go away?"

"Listen. Don't ask me. Say yes."

"Why do you want to go away, Anna?"

"Because, I want to go. Do me the favour."

"Is my lady flying from some danger that threatens her virtue? From some unhappy love?"

"There's something more than my virtue in danger. I am flying from an unhappy love, Cesare," she said gravely, shutting her eyes.

"Heavens! And am I to mix myself up in these tragical complications? No, Anna, no, I sha'n't budge."

"Is there no prayer that can move you. Will you always answer no?"

"I shall always say no."

"Even if I begged you at the point of death?"

"Fortunately your health is excellent," he rejoined, smiling slightly.

"We may all die—from one moment to another," she answered, simply. "Let us go away together, Cesare."

"I have said no, and I mean no, Anna. Don't try to change me. You know it's useless."

"Then will you grant me another favour? This one you will grant."

"Let's hear it."

"Let us go and live alone in the palace in Via Gerolimini."

"In that ugly house?"

"Let us live there alone together."

"Alone? How do you mean?"

"Alone, you and I."

"Without Laura?"

"Without Laura."

"Ah," he said.

She looked at him pleadingly, and in her brown eyes he must have been able to read the sorrowful truth. But he had no pity; he would not spare her the bitter confession of it.

"Be frank," he said, with some severity. "You wish to separate from your sister!"

"Yes."

"And why? Tell me the reason."

"I can't tell you. I wish to separate from Laura."

"When?"

"At once. To-day."

"Indeed? Have you had a quarrel? I'll be peacemaker."

"I doubt it," she said, with a strange smile.

"If you'll tell me what you've quarrelled about, I'll make peace between you."

"But why do you ask these questions and make these offers? I want to separate from my sister. That is all."

"And I don't wish to," he said, looking coldly into his wife's eyes.

"You don't wish to be parted from Laura!" she cried, feeling her feet giving way beneath her.

"I don't indeed."

"Then I will go away myself, she cried, her brain reeling.

"Do as you like," he answered, calmly.

"Oh, heaven help me," she murmured, under her breath, staggering, losing all her strength.

"Now we have come to the fainting-fit," said Cesare, looking at her scornfully, "and so will end this scene of stupid jealousy."

"What jealousy! Who has spoken of jealousy?" she asked haughtily.

"Must I inform you that you have done nothing else for the past half-hour! It strikes me that you have lost the little good sense you ever had.

And I give you notice that I'm not going to make myself ridiculous on your account."

"You wish to stay with Laura!"

"Not only I, but you too. For the sake of the world's opinion, as well as for our own sakes, we can't desert the girl. She's been confided to our protection. It would be a scandal which I'll not permit you to make. If I have to suffer a hundred deaths, I'll not allow you to make a scandal. Do you understand!"

She looked at him, changing colour, feeling that her last hope was escaping her.

"And then," he went on, "I don't know your reasons for not wishing to live any longer with your sister. She's good, she's well-behaved, she's serious; she gives you no trouble; you have no right to find fault with her. It's one of your whims—it's your everlasting desire to be unhappy. Anyhow, your idiotic caprice will soon enough be gratified. Laura will soon be married."

"Do you wish Laura to marry!"

"I wish it earnestly."

"You'll be glad of it!"

"Most glad," he answered, smiling.

Ah, in the days of her womanly innocence, before her mind had been opened to the atrocious revelations of their treason, she would not have understood the import of that answer and that smile; but she knew now the whole depth of human wickedness. He smiled, and curled his handsome black moustaches. Anna lost her head.

"Then you are more infamous than Laura," she cried.

"The vocabulary of Othello," he cried, calmly. "But, you know, it has been proved that Othello was epileptic."

"And he killed Desdemona," said Anna.

"Does it strike you that I look like Desdemona?"

"Not you, not you."

"And who then?"

"Laura."

"Your folly is becoming dangerous, Anna."

"Imminently, terribly dangerous, Cesare."

"Fortunately you take it out in words, not in actions," he concluded, smiling.

She wrung her hands.

"Last night Laura owed her life to a miracle," she said.

"But what has been going on here?" he exclaimed, agitated, rising to his feet. "And where is Laura?"

"Oh, fear nothing, fear nothing on her account. I've not harmed her. She's alive. She's well. She's very well. No wrinkle troubles her beauty, no anxiety disturbs her mind. Fear nothing. She is a sacred person. Your love protects her. Listen, Cesare; she was here last night alone in this room with me; and I had over her the right given me by heaven, given me by men; and I *did not kill her.*"

Cesare had turned slightly pale; that was all.

"And if it is permitted to talk in your own high-sounding rhetoric, what was the ground of your right to kill her?" he asked, looking at the handle of his walking-stick, and emphasising the disdainful *you.*[F]

"Laura has betrayed me. She's in love with you."

"Nothing but this was lacking! That Laura should be in love with me! I'm glad to hear it. You are sure of it? It's an important matter for my vanity. Are you sure of it?"

"Don't jeer at me, Cesare. You don't realise what you are doing. Don't smile like that. Don't drive me to extremes."

"There are two of you in love with me—for I suppose you still love me, don't you? It's a family misfortune. But since you both adore me, it's probably not my fault."

"Cesare, Cesare!"

"And confess that I did nothing to win you."

"You have betrayed me, Cesare. You are in love with Laura."

"Are you sure of it?"

"Sure, Cesare."

"But bear in mind that certainties are somewhat rare in this world. For the past few minutes I've been examining myself, to discover if indeed I had in my soul a guilty passion for Laura. Perhaps I am mad about her, without knowing it. But you, who are an expert in these affairs, you are sure of it. Have the goodness to explain to me, oh, passionate Signora Dias, in what manner I have betrayed you, loving your sister. Describe to me the whole blackness of my treason. Tell me in what my—infamy—consists. Wasn't it infamy you called it? I'm not learned in the language of the heart."

"Oh, God! oh, God!" sobbed Anna, her face buried in her hands, horrified at what she heard and saw.

"I hope we've not to pass the morning invoking the Lord, the Virgin, and the Saints. What do you suppose they care for your idiocy, Anna? They are too wise; and I should be wiser if I cared nothing for it, either. But when your rhetoric casts a slur upon others, it can't be overlooked. I beg you, Signora Dias, to do your husband the kindness of stating your accusations precisely. Set forth the whole atrocity of his conduct. I fold my hands, and sit here on this chair like a king on his judgment-seat. I wait, only adding that you have already used up a good deal of my patience."

"But has Laura told you nothing?"

"Nothing, my dear lady."

"Where is she?"

"She's gone to church, I hear."

"Quietly gone to church?"

"Do you fancy that all women dance in perpetual convulsions to the tune of their sentiments, Signora Dias? No, for the happiness of men, no. Our dear and wise Minerva has gone to mass, for to-day is Sunday."

"With that horrible sin on her conscience! Does she think she can lie even to God? But it's a sacrilege."

"Ah, we're to have a mystical drama, a passion-play now, are we? Dear lady, I see that you have nothing to say to me, and I make my adieux."

He started to go, but she barred the way to him.

"Don't go, Cesare; don't leave me. Since you will have it so, you shall hear from my lips, though they tremble with horror in pronouncing it, the story of your infamy. I will repeat it to you to-day as I repeated it to Laura last night; and I hope it may burn in your heart as it burns in mine. Ah, you laugh; you have the boldness to laugh. You treat this talk as a joke. You sneer at my anger. You would like to get away from me. I annoy you. My voice wearies you. And what I have to say to you will perhaps bring a blush of shame even to your face, corrupt man that you are. But you cannot leave me. You are obliged to remain here. You must give me an account of your betrayal. Ah, don't smile, don't smile; that will do no good; your smile can't turn me aside. I won't allow you to leave me. Remember, Cesare, remember what you did last evening. Remember and be ashamed. Remember how cruel, how wicked, how atrocious it was, what happened last evening between you and my sister. Under my eyes Cesare, and for long minutes, so that I could have no doubt. I could not imagine that I was mad or dreaming. I saw it all, my ears heard the words you spoke, the sound of your kisses, your long kisses. I could not doubt. Oh, how horrible it is for a woman who loves to see the proof that she is betrayed! What new, unknown capacities for sorrow open in her soul! Oh, what have you done to me, Cesare, you whom I adored! You and my sister Laura, what have you done to me!"

She fell into a chair, crushing her temples between her hands.

"Is it your habit to listen at doors? It's not considered good form," said Cesare coldly.

"Do you wish me to die, Cesare? How could you forget that I loved you, that I had given you my youth, my beauty, all my heart, all my soul, that I adored you with every breath, that you alone were the reason for my being? You have forgotten all this, forgotten that I live only for you, my love—you have forgotten it?"

"These sentiments do you honour, though they're somewhat exaggerated. Buy a book of manners, and learn that it's not the thing to listen at doors."

"It was my right to listen, do you understand? I was defending my love, my happiness, my all; but the terrible thing I saw has destroyed for ever everything I cared for."

"Did you really see such a terrible thing?" he asked, smiling.

"If I should live a thousand years, nothing could blot it from my mind. Oh, I shall die, I shall die; I can only forget it by dying."

"You are suffering from cerebral dilatation. It was nothing but a harmless scene of gallantry—it was a jest, Anna."

"Laura said that she loved you. I heard her."

"Of course, girls of her age always say they're in love."

"She kissed you, Cesare. I saw her."

"And what of that? Girls of her age are fond of kissing. They're none the worse for it."

"She was in your arms, Cesare, and for so long a time that to me it seemed a century."

"It's not a bad place, you know, Signora Dias," he responded, smiling.

"Oh, how low, how monstrous! And you, Cesare, you told her that you loved her. I heard you."

"A man always loves a little the woman that is with him. Besides, I couldn't tell her that I hated her; it would scarcely have been polite. I know my book of manners. There's at least one member of our family who preserves good form."

"Cesare, you kissed her."

"I'd defy you to have done otherwise, if you'd been a man. You don't understand these matters."

"On the lips, Cesare."

"It's my habit. It's not a custom of my invention, either. It's rather old. I suspect it took its rise with Adam and Eve."

"But she's a young girl, an innocent young girl, Cesare."

"Girls are not so innocent as they used to be, Anna. I assure you the world is changing."

"She is my sister, Cesare."

"That's a circumstance quite without importance. Relationship counts for nothing."

She looked at him with an expression of intense disgust.

"You, then, Cesare," she said, "have no sense of the greatness of this infamy. She at least, Laura, the other guilty person, turned pale, was troubled, trembled with passion and with terror. You—no! Here you have been for an hour absolutely imperturable; not a shade of emotion has crossed your brazen face; your voice hasn't changed; you feel no fear, no love, no shame; you are not even surprised. She at least shuddered and cried out; she is an Acquaviva! It is true that, though she saw my anger and my despair, she had neither pity nor compunction, but her passion for you, at least, was undisguised. She had feeling, strength, will. But you—no. You, like her, indeed, could see me weep my heart out, could see me convulsed by the most unendurable agony, and have not an ounce of pity for me; but your hardness does not spring, like hers, from love; no, no; from icy indifference. You are as heartless as a tombstone. She, at least, has the courage, the audacity, the effrontery of her wickedness; she declares boldly that she loves you, that she adores you, that she will never cease to love you, that she will always adore you. She is my sister. In her heart there is the same canker that is in mine—a canker from which we are both dying.

You—no! Love? Passion? Not even an illusion. Nothing but a harmless scene of gallantry! A half-hour of amusing flirtation, without consequence! But what does it mean, then, to say that we love? Is it a lie that a man feels justified in telling any woman? And what is a kiss? A fugitive contact of the lips, immediately forgotten? So many false kisses are given in the course of a day and night! Nonsense, triviality, rubbish! It's bad form to spy at doors; its exaggeration to call a thing infamous; it's madness to be jealous. And the sin that you have committed, instead of originating in passion, which might in some degree excuse it, you reduce to an every-day vulgarity, a commonplace indecency; my sister becomes a vulgar flirt, you a vulgar seducer, and I a vulgar termagant screaming out her morbid jealousy. The whole affair falls into the mud. My sister's guilty love, your caprice, my despair, all are in the mud, among the most disgusting human garbage, where there is no spiritual light, no cry of sorrow, where everything is permissible, where the man expires and the beast triumphs. Do you know what you are, Cesare?"

"No, I don't know. But if you can tell me, I shall be indebted for the favour."

"You are a man without heart, without conscience; a soul without greatness and without enthusiasm; you are a lump of flesh, exhausted by unworthy pleasures and morbid desires. You are a ruin, in heart, in mind, in senses; you belong to the class of men who are rotten; you fill me with fright and with pity. I did not know that I was giving my hand to a corpse scented with heliotrope, that I was uniting my life to the mummy of a gentleman, whose vitiated senses could not be pleased by a young, beautiful, and loving wife, but must crave her sister, her pure, chaste, younger sister! Have you ever loved, Cesare? Have you ever for a moment felt the immensity of real love? In your selfishness you have made an idol of yourself, an idol without greatness. A thing without viscera, without pulses, without emotion! You are corrupt, perverted, depraved, even to the point of betraying your wife who adores you, with her sister whom you do not love! Ah, you are a coward, a dastard; that's what you are, a dastard!"

She wrung her hands and beat her temples, pacing the room as a madwoman paces her cell. But not a tear fell from her eyes, not a sob issued from her breast.

He stood still, his face impenetrable; not one of her reproaches had brought a trace of colour to it. She threw herself upon a sofa, exhausted; but her eyes still burned and her lips trembled.

"Now that you have favoured me with so amiable a definition of myself," said he, "permit me to attempt one of you."

His tone was so icy, he pronounced the words so slowly, that Anna knew he was preparing a tremendous insult. Instinctively, obeying the blind anger of her love, she repeated, "You are a dastard; that's what you are, a dastard."

"My dear, you are a bore—that's what *you* are."

"What do you say?" she asked, not understanding.

"You're a bore, my dear."

The insult was so atrocious, that for the first time in the course of their talk her eyes filled with tears, and a sigh burst from her lips—lips that were purple, like those of a dying child. It seemed as if something had broken in her heart.

"Nothing but a bore. I don't employ high-sounding words, you see. I speak the plain truth. You're a bore."

Another sigh, a sigh of insupportable physical pain, as if the hard word *bore* had cut her flesh, like a knife.

"You flatter yourself that you're a woman of grand passions," he went on, after looking at his watch, and giving a little start of surprise to see how much time he had wasted here. "No? You flatter yourself that you're a creature of impulse, a woman with a fate, a woman destined to a tragic end; and to satisfy this notion, you complicate and embroil and muddle up your own existence, and mortally bore those who are about you. With your rhetoric, your tears, your sobs, your despair, your interminable letters, your livid face and your gray lips, you're enough to bore the very saints in heaven."

He pretended not to see her imploring eyes, which had suddenly lost their anger, and were craving mercy.

"Remember all the stupidities you've committed in the past four or five years," he went on, "and all the annoyance you've given us. You were a handsome girl, rich, with a good name. You might have married any one of a dozen men of your own age, your own rank, gentlemen, who were in love with you. That would have been sensible, orderly; you would have been as happy as happy can be. But what! Anna Acquaviva, the romantic heroine, condescend to be happy! No, no. That were beneath her! So you had to fancy yourself in love with a beggar whom you couldn't marry."

She made a gesture, as if to defend Giustino Morelli.

"Oh, did you really love him? Thanks for the compliment; you're charming this morning. Passion, inequality of position, drama, flight into Egypt, fortunately without a child—forgive the impropriety, but it escaped me. Morelli, chancing to be a decent fellow, Morelli ran away, poor devil! and our heroine treated herself to the luxury of a mortal illness. We, Laura, I, everybody, were bored by the flight, bored by the illness. The lesson was a severe one, and most women would have been cured of their inclination towards the theatrical, as well as of their scarlet fever. But not so Anna Acquaviva. It didn't matter to her that she had risked her reputation, her honour; it didn't matter to her that she had staked the name of her family; all this only excited her imagination. And, behold, she begins her second romance, her second drama, her second tragedy, and enter upon the scene, to be bored to death, Signor Cesare Dias!"

"Oh, Holy Virgin, help me," murmured Anna, pressing her hands to her temples.

"Dramatic love for Cesare Dias, an old man, a man who has never gone in for passion, who doesn't wish to go in for it, who is tired of all such bothersome worries. Anna Acquaviva gives herself up to an unrequited love, 'one of the most desolating experiences of the soul'—that's a phrase I found in one of your letters. Desolation, torture, spasms, despair, bitterness, these are the words which our ill-fated heroine, Anna Acquaviva, employs to depict her condition to herself and to others. And Cesare Dias, who had arranged his life in a way not to be bored and not to bore anyone, Cesare Dias, who is an entirely common and ordinary person, happy in his mediocrity, suddenly finds himself against his will dragged upon the scene as hero! He is the man of mysteries, the man who will not love or who loves another, the superior man, the neighbour of the stars. And nevertheless we find a means of boring him."

"Ah, Cesare, Cesare, Cesare!" she said, beseeching compassion.

"Imbecile ought to be added to the name of Cesare Dias. That's the title which I best deserve. Only an imbecile—and I was one for half-an-hour—could have ceded to your sentimental hysterics. I was an imbecile. But to let you die, to complete your tragedy of unrequited love——"

"Oh, why didn't you let me die?" she cried.

"I believe it would have been as well for many of us. What a comfort for you, dear heroine, to die consumed by an unhappy passion! Gaspara Stampa, Properzia de' Rossi, and other illustrious ladies of ancient times, with whose names you have favoured me in your letters, would have found their imitator. I'm sure you would have died blessing me."

Bowing her head, she sighed deeply, as if she were indeed dying.

"Instead of letting you die, I went through the dismal farce of marrying you. And I assure you that I've never ceased to regret it. I regretted it the very minute after I'd made you my idiotic proposal. Ah, well, every man has his moments of inexplicable weakness, and he pays dearly for them. And marriage, alas, hasn't proved a sentimental comedy. With your pretentions to passion, to love, to mutual adoration, you've bored me even more than I expected."

"But what, then, is marriage from your point of view?" she cried.

"A bothersome obligation, when a man marries a woman like you."

"You would have preferred my sister?" she asked, exasperated. But she was at once sorry for this vulgarity; and he speedily punished it.

"Yes, I should have preferred your sister. She's not a bore. I find her extremely diverting."

"She loved you from the beginning," she says. "A pity she didn't tell you so."

"A pity. I assure you I should have married her."

"Ah, very well."

But suddenly she raised her eyes to her husband; and at the sight of that beloved person her courage failed her. She took his hand, and said, "Ah, Cesare, Cesare, you are right. But I loved you, I loved you, and you have deceived me with my sister."

"Signora Dias, you have rather a feeble memory," he returned, icily, drawing his hand away.

"How do you mean?"

"I mean that you easily forget. We are face to face; you can't lie. Have I ever told you that I loved you?"

"No—never," she admitted, closing her eyes agonised to have to admit it.

"Have I ever promised to love you?"

"No—never."

"Well, then, according to the laws of love, I've not deceived you, my dear Anna. My heart has never belonged to you, therefore it's not been taken from you. I promised nothing, therefore I owe you nothing."

"It's true. You're right, Cesare," she said; draining this new cup of bitterness that he had distilled for her.

"Perhaps you will speak to me of the laws of the land. Very good; according to the law a man and wife are required to be mutually faithful. A magistrate would say that I had betrayed you. But consider a little. Make an effort of memory, Anna, and recall the agreement I proposed to you that evening at Sorrento, before committing my grand blunder. I told you that I wished to remain absolutely free, free as a bachelor; and you consented. Is it true or not true?"

"It is true. I consented."

"I told you that I would tolerate no interference on your part with my relations with other women; and remember, Anna, you consented. Is that true or untrue?"

"It is true," she said, feeling that she was falling into an abyss.

"You see, therefore, that neither according to the laws of love nor according to the laws of marriage have I betrayed you. And if you had a conscience, to adopt your own phraseology, if you had the least loyalty, you would at once confess that I have not betrayed you. You accepted the whole bargain. I am free in heart, and at liberty to do as I like. I have not betrayed you. Confess it."

"Cesare, Cesare, be human, be Christian; don't require me to say that."

"Tragedies are one thing, and truth is another, Anna. I desire to establish the fact that I haven't betrayed you, my dear. For what I did last night, for what I may have done on any other night, for what I may do any night in the future, I have your own permission. Confess it."

"I can't say that, do you understand?" she cried. "Oh, you are always in the right; you always know how to put yourself in the right. You are right in your selfishness, in your perfidy, in your wickedness, in your frightful corruption; you were right in proposing that disgraceful bargain to me, which I was not ashamed to accept, and which you to-day so justly and so appropriately remind me of. But I believed that to love, to adore a man as I loved and adored you, would be a charm to conquer with; and I have lost. For you are stronger than I; indifference is stronger than love; selfishness is stronger than passion. Generous abandonment cannot overcome the refined calculation of a corrupt man. I am wrong, I alone, I confess it—since I loved you to the point of dying for you, since I imagined that that was enough, since I had in my soul the divine hope of winning you by my love. I am wrong, I confess it; yes, I confess it. I cannot love nor hate nor live. I am nothing but a bore, a superfluous person, and a tiresome; it is true; it is true. Say it again."

"If you wish it, I will."

"You are right. You are always right. I have done nothing but blunder. I have always obeyed the mad impulses of my heart. I fled from my home. I ought not to have loved you, and I loved you. I loved you; I have bored you; and I myself, of my free will, gave you permission to betray me. You are the most vicious man I know. You're unredeemed by a thought or a feeling. You horrify me. Under the same roof with your wife, you have committed an odious sin—a sin that would make the worst men shudder. And I can't punish you, because I consented to it; because I debased the dignity of my love before you; because indeed I am a cowardly and infamous creature. See how right you are! You have sinned, but so far as I am concerned you are innocent. I am infamous and cowardly, because I ought to have died rather than accept that loathsome bargain. Forgive me if I have upbraided you. I'll ask Laura's pardon too. No human being is soiled with an infamy so great as mine. Forgive me."

Perhaps he felt in these words the confusion of madness; perhaps he saw the light of madness in her eyes. But he was unmoved. She was a woman who had led him into committing a folly, who had bored him, and, what was more, who would like to continue to bore him in the future. He was unmoved. He was glad to have got the better of her in this struggle. He was unmoved. He thought it time to leave her, if he would retain his advantage.

"Good-bye, Anna," he said, rising.

"Don't go away, don't go away," she cried, throwing herself before him.

"Do you imagine that this duet is pleasing?" he asked, drawing on his gloves. "For the rest, we've said all there is to say. I can't think you have any more insults to favour me with."

"You hate me, do you?"

"No, I don't hate you exactly."

"Don't go away. Don't go away. I must tell you something very serious."

"Good-bye, Anna," he repeated, moving towards the door.

"Cesare, if you go away, I shall do something desperate," she cried, convulsively tearing her hair.

"You'd be incapable. To do anything desperate one must have talent. And you're a fool," he replied, smiling ironically.

"Cesare, if you go away, I shall die."

"Bah, bah, you'll not die. To die one must have courage." And he opened the door and went out.

She ran to the threshold. He was already at a distance. She heard the street door close behind him. For a few minutes she stood there, fearing to move lest she should fall; then mechanically she turned back. She went to her looking-glass, repaired the disorder of her hair, and put on a hat, a black veil, and a sealskin cloak. She forgot nothing. Her pocket-handkerchief was in her muff; in her hand she carried her card-case of carved Japanese ivory.

At last she left her room, and entered her husband's. A servant was putting it in order; but, seeing his mistress, he bowed and took himself off. She was alone there, in the big brown chamber, in the gray winter daylight. She went to her husband's desk, and sat down before it, as if she were going to write. But, after a moment's thought, she did not write. She opened a drawer, took something from it, and concealed it in her pocket.

After that, she passed through the house and out into the street.

She crossed the Piazza Vittoria, and entered the Villa Nazionale. Children were playing by the fountain, and she stopped for a moment to look at them. Twice she made the tour of the Villa; then she looked at her watch; then she seated herself on one of the benches. There were very few people abroad. The damp earth was covered with dead leaves.

She fixed her eyes upon the dial of her watch, counting the minutes and the seconds. All at once she put her hand into her pocket, and felt the thing that she had hidden there.

Anna rose. It was two o'clock.

She left the Villa, walking towards the Chiatamone. Before the door of a little house in the Via del Chiatamone she stopped. She hesitated for a moment; then she lifted the bronze knocker, and let it fall.

The door was opened by Luigi Caracciolo.

He did not speak. He took her hand, and drew her into the house.

They crossed two antechambers, hung with old tapestries, ornamented with ancient and modern arms, and with big Delft vases filled with growing palms, a smoking-room furnished with rustic Swiss chairs and tables, and entered a drawing-room. The curtains were drawn, the lamps lighted. The floor and the walls were covered with Oriental carpets; the room was full of beautiful old Italian furniture, statues, pictures, bronzes. There were many flowers about, red and white roses, subtly perfumed.

Caracciolo took a bunch of roses, and gave them to Anna.

"Dear Anna—my dear love," he said.

A faint colour came to her cheeks.

"What is it? Tell me, Anna. Dear one, dear one!"

"Don't speak to me like that," she said.

"Do I offend you? I can't think that I offend you—I who feel for you the deepest tenderness, the most absolute devotion."

He took her hands.

"It is dark here," she said.

"The day was so sad, the daylight was so melancholy. I have waited for you so many hours, Anna."

"I have come, you see."

"Thank you for having remembered your faithful servant." And delicately he kissed her gloved hand.

"Why not open the curtains a little?" she asked.

He drew aside his curtains, and let in the ashen light. She went to the window, and looked out upon the sea.

"Anna, Anna, come away. Somebody might see you."

"It doesn't matter."

"But I can't allow you to compromise yourself, Anna; I love you too much."

"I have come here to compromise myself," she said.

"Then—you love me a little?" he demanded, trying to draw her away from the window.

She did not answer. She sat down in an arm-chair.

"Tell me that you love me a little, Anna."

"I don't love you."

"Dear Anna, dear Anna," he murmured with his caressing voice, "how can I believe you, since you are here. Tell me that you love me a little. For three years I have waited for that word. Dear Anna, sweet Anna, you know that I have adored you for so long a time. Anna, Anna!"

"What has happened was bound to happen," she said.

"Anna, I conjure you,[G] tell me that you love me."

She shuddered as she heard him use the familiar pronoun.

"Do you love me?"

"I don't know. I know nothing."

"Dear one, dear one," he murmured, trembling with hope, in an immense transport of love.

He drew nearer to her and kissed her on the cheek.

A cry of pain burst from her, and she sprang up, horrified, terrified, and tried to leave the room.

"Oh, for mercy's sake, forgive me. Don't go away. Anna, Anna, forgive me if I have offended you. I love you so! If you go away I shall die."

"People don't die for such slight things."

"People die of love."

"Yes. But one must have courage to die."

"Don't let us talk of these dismal things. My love, we mustn't talk of things that will sadden you. Your beautiful face is troubled. Tell me that you forgive me. Do you forgive me?"

"I forgive you."

"I don't believe it. You don't forgive me. You love another."

"No, no—no other."

"And Cesare?"

But scarcely had he spoken the fatal name when he saw his error. Her eyes blazed; she trembled from head to foot, in a nervous convulsion.

"Listen," she said. "If you have a heart, if you have any pity, if you wish me to stay here with you, never name him again, never name him."

"You are right." But then he added, "And yet you loved him, you love him still."

"No. I love no one any more."

"Why would you not accept me when I proposed for you?"

"Because."

"Why did you marry that old man?"

"Because."

"And now why do you love him? Why do you love him?"

"I don't know."

"You see, you do love him," he cried in despair.

"Oh, God, oh, God!" she sobbed.

"Oh, I am a fool. Forgive me, forgive me. But I love you, and I lose my head. I love you, and I am desperate. And I need to know if you still love him. You will always love him? Is it so?"

"Till death," she said, with a strange look and accent.

"Say it again."

"Till death," she repeated, with the same strange intonation.

They were silent.

Luigi Caracciolo put his arm round her waist, and drew her slowly towards him.

Her eyes were fixed and void. She did not feel his arms about her. She did not feel his kisses. He kissed her hair, he kissed her sweet white throat, he kissed her little rosy ear. Anna was absorbed in a desperate meditation, far from all human things. He kissed her face, her eyes, her lips; she did not know it. But suddenly she felt his embrace become closer, stronger; she heard his voice change, it was no longer tender and caressing, it was fervid with tumultuous passion, it uttered confused delirious words. Silently, looking at him with burning eyes, she tried to disengage herself.

"Let me go," she said.

"Anna, Anna, I love you so—I have loved you so long!"

"Let me go, let me go!"

"You are my adored one—I adore you above all things."

"Let me go. You horrify me."

He let her go.

"But what have you come here for?" he asked, sorrowfully.

"I have come to commit an infamy."

"Anna, Anna, you are killing me!"

She looked at him fixedly.

"What is it, Anna? Something is troubling you, and you won't tell me what it is. My poor friend! You have come here with an anguish in your heart, wishing to escape from it; you have come here to weep; and I have behaved like a brute, a blackguard."

"No, you are good, I shall remember you," and she gave him her hand.

"Don't go away. Tell me first what it is. Tell me what you came for. Tell me, dearest Anna."

"It's too long a story, too long," she said, as if in a dream, passing her hand over her brow. "And now I must go, I must go."

"No, stop here, talk to me, weep. It will do you good."

"I can't."

"Why?"

"My minutes are numbered. You'll understand some day—to-morrow. Now I must go."

"Anna, how can I let you go like this? You have come here to be comforted, and I have treated you shamefully. Forgive me."

"You are not to blame, not in the least."

"But what is it that you are in trouble about, Anna? Who has been making you miserable, my poor fond soul? Whose fault is it? Who is to blame? Cesare?"

"No, I am to blame, I only."

"And Cesare—you admit it."

"No."

"Cesare is an infamous scoundrel, and I know it," he exclaimed.

"It is I who am infamous."

"I don't believe you. I should believe no one who said that, Anna."

"I must be infamous, since I alone am unhappy. I must go."

"Will you come back?—to-morrow? Anna, you are so sad, you are in such distress, I can't let you go."

"No one can detain me, no one."

"Anna, forget that I have spoken to you of love."

"I have forgotten it. Good-bye."

"You musn't go like this. You are too much agitated."

"No, I am calm. Listen, will you do me a favour? You repeated some verses to me one evening at Sorrento—some French verses—do you remember?"

"Yes. Baudelaire's '*Harmonie du Soir*,'" he answered, surprised by her question.

"Have you the volume?"

"Yes."

"Take it, and copy that poem for me. Afterwards I will say good-bye."

He went into his library and brought back *Les Fleurs du Mal*. He seated himself at his writing-table, and looked at Anna. There was an expression of such immense sorrow in her eyes, that he faltered, and asked, "Shall I write?"

She bowed her head. While he was writing the first lines, Anna turned her back to him. She put her hand into her pocket and brought forth a little shining object of ivory and steel. He in a low voice repeated the verse he was writing—"*Valse mélancolique et langoureux vertige*"—when suddenly there was the report of a pistol, and a little cloud of smoke rose towards the ceiling.

Anna had shot herself through the heart, and fallen to the floor. Her little gloved hand held the revolver that she had taken from the drawer of her husband's desk. Luigi Caracciolo stood rooted to the carpet, believing that he must be mad.

So died Anna Acquaviva, innocent.

FOOTNOTES:

[F] *Voi*, instead of the more familiar *tu*, which he had previously employed.

[G] Having hitherto used the formal *voi*, he now uses the intimate *tu*.

Lightning Source UK Ltd.
Milton Keynes UK
UKHW041009130922
408745UK00001B/156

9 789355 754769